In Praise of
Psychotherapists

In Praise of Psychotherapists

How Change Occurs Despite Baffling
Theory and Bureaucracy

James M. McMahon

Writers Club Press
San Jose New York Lincoln Shanghai

In Praise of Psychotherapists
How Change Occurs Despite Baffling Theory and Bureaucracy

Writers Club Press
an imprint of iUniverse, Inc.

For information address:
iUniverse, Inc.
5220 S. 16th St., Suite 200
Lincoln, NE 68512
www.iuniverse.com

ISBN: 0-595-22635-3

Printed in the United States of America

For my Father, Edward F. McMahon, former Battalion Chief, FDNY, who taught me the dignity of work, and for psychotherapists everywhere.

Contents

Acknowledgments

My wife, Lijuan Niu McMahon, held my hand and my heart throughout this writing. Wilson Carneiro, Jr. provided essential technical support. Paul H. Hebner was a gentle and precise editor and advisor. Sharon Hymer, Sr. Pascal Conforti, OSU and Edward F. McMahon, Jr. were beacons of hope. The many friends and teachers and patients I have been blessed to know over the years live in every page.

The cover photograph shows S. Freud's therapy couch, presently in the Freud Museum, Vienna, and is presented through the generosity of the Freud Museum, London, U.K.

Introduction

My friend, Sr. Pascal, asked me one day over lunch, "So how's the book about psychotherapy coming?" Pascal and I are good buddies and she has been my chief fan since I began writing books a few years ago. She is chaplain at St.Clare's hospital and health care center, a NYC Roman Catholic Archdiocese's major weapon in the fight against AIDS, and as such she is in the "trenches" every day, dealing with the impossible, loving the "unlovable."

I told her I was tired and didn't want to spend time organizing a large amount of material. Actually, I was resisting finishing this project, one I had been working on for the better part of a decade. She told me she hoped I would share the ideas about our work that she and I spoke of all the time. We finished our lunch of laughs and truths and a little gossip at the Afghan restaurant squished in on Ninth Avenue, around the corner from the hospital. We parted with warm feelings.

That night I woke consumed with "the book about psychotherapy." I lay in bed unable to sleep, and then I realized exactly what I wanted to tell my colleagues, colleagues of mine both as patients and therapists. It would not be a long tome. It would not be unnecessarily technical and complicated. I would speak only of what I needed to and what came from my heart. What I needed to say was that psychotherapy works—despite itself. Despite its damaging categorizing of human beings, despite its sometimes arrogant and patronizing attitudes toward its clients, despite its often-obfuscating theories, psychotherapy is an exquisite adventure, unlike anything previously known to humankind. It works because of the intrinsic growth process that gets activated when one person tells his story to another who is devoted to listening and who nourishes these revelations by risking her most intimate self in contact with the other. I have spent my life deeply involved in psychotherapy, on both sides of the couch. It remains to this day my glorious absorption. Here I speak of it, what is magnificent about it, but perhaps even more important, about its intrinsic flaws. For it is terribly flawed, just as we humans are flawed.

There is a chapter in which I cheer therapists on, for despite our arrogance, we are a scared bunch, often shaky and insecure, but for the most part with good hearts. It is those hearts, combined with infinite patience and good will, that make growth possible. I encourage each of us, whether counselors, pastors or psychotherapists, to develop a unique metapsychology, a way of thinking about the world and about personality and about psychological difficulties and about healing, that has our own fingerprints upon it. Read the literature, get good supervision, take seminars; but at the end develop your own perspective. For at the moment of truth it will be you alone who engages your patient. Be absorbed with *him or her*, not the need for approval from psychotherapy's authorities. I show you how I went about it after many years of suffering and trying to be "right." I have no desire that you agree with my way. What I urge is that you courageously—not arrogantly—create your own way.

Another chapter deals with the question of diagnosis and how to distinguish its usefulness from the times, more often I'm sad to say, that it keeps us from knowing and loving our patients better. One of the pitfalls of our profession is that we are encouraged to be "smart." Sometimes we show off a little, and often we silently feel inadequate when we compare ourselves to colleagues who appear to know more than us. "Diagnosing" a patient is a place where this madness can take place, and what suffers is our fresh experience of a fellow human being—our client—across the room from us.

Chapter three addresses the basic fault of the whole enterprise: the presumption intrinsic in many psychotherapeutic denominations that we can cure ourselves primarily through understanding, and that the smartest among us is the best or most effective. Closer to the truth is that we cure others despite our smugness; our love conquers all despite the narcissism that makes psychoanalysis and other approaches often suffer from the very disease they purport to cure. We'll examine the "super-professionalism" that often results in our losing sight of our patients. Finally, we'll look at our own personal tendencies toward hubris as well as the intrinsic difficulties of the task itself. All this makes psychotherapy daunting. But it will not do us in if our hearts are in the right place, and we are capable of a little humility.

The next two chapters have to do with change. This, of course, is what we aim for when we do psychotherapy. But it is a tricky subject, change. For though we may say we want to change, we may not *really* want to, or perhaps we are a little scared of it, or perhaps we don't really need to, anyway. And who is to decide? Since my student days I have wondered about change. God knows I was in need of a lot of it, and I have had many psychotherapies, individual and group, over the years. In these chapters I share my reflections on change, once again, mostly to stimulate your own thinking. I suggest just where in our psyche change actually occurs and also some basic psychological strategies and attitudes that seem to be present in all experiences that result in change, regardless of theoretical orientation. The chapters on change are my take on what really happens between patient and therapist that influences and promotes freedom.

The last chapter is the story of my former patient, Sarah, in whom almost from the inside of a crater during a volcanic eruption of decades of calcified rage and grief and crippling injunctions, I witnessed the thunderous power of spirit over impossible odds. Fortunately, neither Sarah nor I knew that it was impossible, and so she got well.

Sometimes, I use the pronoun "he," sometimes "she," sometimes "ours" and sometimes "yours." Sometimes, I refer to our work as counseling, sometimes psychotherapy or even psychoanalysis. I strive to include all the different aspects of our experience. I choose inclusiveness over editorial consistency. This book is written for the "regular" psychotherapist and counselor, the "grunts in the trenches" who struggle each day to bring their best selves to a difficult task, and also for our patients and clients. It is not written for scholars and theoreticians. It is not about how smart we are, but how wise. It is not about "us" curing "them." It is about how we can listen and love each other and thus unleash growth into the fullness of ourselves. The search for the infinite newness in our being is a most glorious quest. Unfortunately, it is terrifying. But let us keep on trying, you and I, confident that though we are far less than perfect in the search, the result is a little more love and a little more truth.

1

The Grunts in the Trenches

In the Spring of 1992, a 43 year-old woman entered the office of a psychotherapist in Corvallis, Oregon. The woman, severely depressed, had met the psychotherapist, Linda Carrol, at a course taught by her at the local community college. At the end of the first class the woman sat in the back of the class and wept. "'She was so desperate to talk about herself but she couldn't," Ms. Carroll recalled. "I don't think I've ever seen anyone suffering so much from acute depression. She literally could not talk without crying." They made an appointment.

The patient told the therapist that she was Alice Metzinger. Alice lived in Corvallis with her accountant friend of 12 years, Rob Duncan, and her 13 year-old son, Jamie. She had a normal life. She was a respected member of the community. A good neighbor and friend, "a cooking instructor at the local community college, a mom who made cookies for her son's sports team, a jogger seen daily on the path along the Williamette River."

Soon she told Linda Carrol a story she had told no one for 23 years, not her life partner, not her son, not her closest friends. Nor had she been in touch since she was 19 with her mother and father and seven siblings, a very close Irish Catholic family of which she was the oldest. What she revealed to Ms. Carroll was that she was indeed not Alice Metzinger (the name of an infant who had died the year of her own birth) but rather Katherine Ann Power, a former anti-Vietnam war activist who had been on the FBI's most wanted list for 17 years until they removed it for want of any leads to her whereabouts.

Raised a devout and responsible person, the firstborn, a star in her Roman Catholic Prep School in Colorado, Power had traveled to New England to attend Brandeis University on scholarship. These were heady times, and Brandeis was a focal point of the campus demonstrations that were to reach their pinnacle when American troops entered Cambodia in 1970. In her idealism Power joined several student-leaders of the anti-war movement, and together with three ex-convicts on study-parole at the university, a plan was hatched to rob a Boston bank and use the money for anti-war activities. On September 23, 1970 five of the group stole $26,000 from the State Street Bank and Trust Company in Brighton. The first police officer to arrive at the bank, Walter A. Schroeder, was shot in the back by one of the ex-convicts, William Gilday, Jr. Gilday is serving a life sentence for the murder. Power was the driver in an escape vehicle several blocks away.

Thoroughly engaged with each other, Power spoke to Carroll for months of her grief about what happened that day. In the course of the treatment of her depression she made the decision to come out of hiding. Through some adroit legal maneuvering a deal was struck in which she would return to Massachusetts and be sentenced to five years in prison. "My goal was never to turn her in," Ms. Carroll told reporter Timothy Egan. (1) "It was to get her well. What happened with the law was secondary. She started to see her life through the lens of this depression, and when that happened, the fog lifted. She wanted to turn herself in."

On October 6, 1993 she was led, hands in shackles, before Judge Robert Banks of the Suffolk County Superior Court to be sentenced to a pre-arranged eight-to-fifteen years of imprisonment. She would be separated from her husband and son and her friends and her recently reunited parents and siblings for at least five years. Yet she was smiling broadly. I witnessed this scene on TV. Some thought that the smile was proof of her depraved indifference to the murder of an innocent, good man. They thought the sentence much too lenient, especially in the light of her "attitude."

The truth about her attitude was revealed, with Powers' permission, by her psychotherapist. " I saw her walk before that judge with a smile on her face and it was the first time I had ever seen her smile. She had found some peace and resolution of an impossible problem, and I broke down in tears."

I did, too. It was a day I was proud to be a psychotherapist. This simple, journey-person "shrink" in a small town in the far West of our country had made true contact with a fellow human being and in doing so saved a life with compassion and dignity and skill. It was a good day, that day, to be a psychotherapist. And this is the truth of our profession: the miracles of change occur in the perseverance of the toilers in the field, the grunts in the trenches. The princes among us in the universities and psychoanalytic think tanks have their place. But it is in Oregon and the quiet offices of the quiet towns and big cities throughout the land where contact is made that healing—mostly unnoticed and unacknowledged—takes place. And daily. Daily, depression is faced squarely and without fear; anxiety is compassionately born; the anguish of couples is gently surfaced; the terror at being alive, and the despair at being alive while not feeling worthy are allowed, accepted and healed. So why do we not love ourselves more? Why do we psychotherapists worry and anguish and rarely celebrate ourselves and each other ? Why are we embarrassed by our uniqueness; our 'strange' urge to engage another, and in our own way?

I suspect that too many of us in our profession suffer too much and too long. We feel inadequate, fakes, when compared to the standards presented to us. That certainly is true of my students. And so we *do* fake it, not because we are fakes, but because we do not believe it to be permissible to be ourselves. We are fused with the expectations of our leaders. We are suffering from the same thing we are helping our patients to transcend. We have not been taught that we are heroes. I plan to remind you therapists of that and your patients and friends, too, though there are many ways we need to clean up our act.

I confess that for most of my professional life I have felt somewhat stupid. I always suspected, as people declaimed heartily about theory, that they all knew something that I didn't. I tried to fake it, and perhaps nobody noticed, but when I got home I was often upset. I knew I was reasonably intelligent. My performance was erratic from time to time due to my own psychological problems but by and large I was able to function well intellectually. I often had original ideas about things. I made some good interpretations, ones that seemed to rock the status quo that resided in my patient's psyche. I had a fair sense of what dreams communicated. I was blessed with a very good memory for what happened between someone and myself if true intimacy had transpired, even though I might not remember the person's name. (Once, in the subway, I ran into a former patient whom I had not seen in twelve years. We greeted each other and I inquired about his wife. He asked me about some members of a group he had attended. As he dashed off the train at his stop I remembered the first dream he had ever told me. But for the life of me I couldn't remember his name!)

I know now that much of what I remember is organized around affect and visual perception, not cognitive information or facts. That's just the way my mind works. It reminds me of Ernst Schachtel's classic article in which he points out the difference between the proximity senses and the distance senses. The proximity senses, organized around smell and taste and touch and odor, characterize the early years of a child's life. As language and independence develop, the distance senses, vision and hearing, serve more as the anchors of memory. This explained infantile amnesia for Schachtel, (2) not a nuclear bomb-like repression as Freud maintained.

I remember how excited I was when I read this. It was so brilliant. It lit up my mind. Somehow I was refreshed by it, as well. I don't know exactly why. Perhaps it was because it challenged the orthodox metapsychology. But it was not just that it was rebellious. It was because I was watching a man think his own thoughts and come up with a refreshingly new and brilliant framework. And one that I didn't have to restrict my own spirit to grasp. I never became a true believer of the interpersonal school, either. But I was always partial to the voices in the wilderness, like Schactel or Gregory Bateson, who came at reality not from a conceptual framework so much as from their own internal vision.

For me, anyhow, my memories seemed to be organized differently from many of my colleagues, at least those who spoke at conferences and colloquia and professional meetings. I no longer feel so inadequate about that, but I did for a long time. Yet my patients seemed to get better. Little by little I let myself question the way things were in the psychoanalytic body politic. I was gradually separating from the fusion of those whose manifest goal, ironically, was psychological separation. I began to find my own way. *I began to realize that growing out into oneself was the result of appreciating the value of your own ideas and perceptions, combined with the bravery of making true emotional contact with another.*

In this meditation on our work I want to encourage you to find your own way, clearly, publicly, and without apology. You have studied hard; you have earned your degrees; you have suffered the terrors of your own psychotherapy. And most important, you have lived! Don't ignore what you have learned in school, and don't disregard the guidance of those with more experience. But always remember that nobody knows what you know; nobody processes the world exactly as you do. You are the only one of *you* in the whole history of the universe. You have an original and unique tale to tell. What is required here is true humility. Humility is not humiliation nor a false modesty. In its Latin root ("of the earth") it means being what you are and accepting who you are. This includes all of you, your strengths as well as those aspects of yourself that may be average. Finding your own way and making an unapologetic stand for your personal vision is not cocky or grandiose. It merely is an assertion of what is. It is not narcissism but rather an abnegation of childish fusion.

In this book, I will show you some of my journey. I do this not to suggest that you should accept my journey or any part of it as yours, but just to show you one man's journey. Hopefully, there will be things that you will find helpful to you and your work as it would be helpful to me if I had a chance to learn about your journey. The important thing as you read this book is to know that it is all right to have your own journey. You needn't be a slave to anyone else's notion of how you should do things. I want to encourage you to be your own person both as a psychotherapist and in life in general. If you get encouragement in this I will have accomplished most of what I am attempting to do.

I begin by sketching for you my personal metapsychology. Each of our personal metapsychologies is to be co-created with the past. You will see that mine is a kind of "attachment theory," but most of it was created out of my own experience, my own contacts—with others, with life, with myself. There is of course, overlap with viewpoints of others. After all, truth is truth, reality is reality, and when you focus in on your angle on it, some one else will have been there as well. The important thing is that it is yours, not the automatic application of an "accepted" point of view. Don't eschew formal training, just don't get emotionally and spiritually lost in it. Underneath it all you are probably doing what you really believe anyway, although you might not even be entirely conscious of it yourself. If your patients are lucky you will be helping them by the application of your truths. And if they are really lucky you will be enjoying yourself at the same time.

Question everything, not in a wasteful rebelliousness, but rather in a cooperative individuality. In the next chapter I even question the reality of psychopathology. Following that, I offer you the opportunity to see that psychoanalytic psychotherapy, as magnificent and helpful as it is, often suffers from the same illness it purports to cure, namely, an overweening self-centeredness, narcissism. I remind us that anything which gets between us and our patients—be it metapsychology, diagnosis, sophisticated theories of personality or treatment or even an over-professional demeanor—limits contact and engagement and consequently limits the possibility of growth. Relatedness in an ambience of radical self-accept-ance is a *sine qua non* for growth. Not even "unconditional positive regard," which is subtly patronizing, does the trick. What is needed is *true emotional contact, an intimacy where both reach deep within to their inner-most selves and strive to offer it to the other.* Such contact is between equals. And it is this contact that elicits expansion.

One needs courage to be a psychotherapist. She needs courage to face the onslaught of the attacks by her patients and their unconscious, his-torical agendas. She needs courage to live in a climate of criticism, jokes, and sometimes downright hostility toward her profession and to herself, a practitioner. She needs courage even more to be willing to engage the eruptions of her inner processes as these are elicited by her patients, as they inevitably will be. This happens to everyone in the course of living, but the psychotherapist places herself in a situation each day where the whole point of the enterprise is to witness such eruptions, both hers and her patients, and to skillfully find a way to put them to good use. And in these political and economic times we must also struggle with the ran-dom approaches to solve our medical financial crisis. These approaches by folks not knowledgeable about psychotherapy, or actually hostile to it, put yet another serious pressure on her, viz., financial insecurity. On top of all of this she must resist the enormous pressures of the psychothera-peutic bureaucracy itself, which ironically, much as the managed care cabal, tends to limit the ways the psychotherapist can listen to her call to see and hear and feel the world in her own way, and in so doing provide the possibility for those who consult her to find their own way (more about this in chapter 3).

She is strangled by all these pressures. How to be herself in the midst of all of this? And her own narcissism, of course, is always lurking in the wings, tempting her to sidestep the problem of malignant professionalism by malignant self-centeredness and grandiosity. "If you can't lick 'em, join 'em" it tempts. We who have chosen the pursuit of truth, no holds barred, joust daily with the impulse to capitulate, to be engulfed by bureaucracy, to be politically correct, to avoid the risky, and in doing so, sabotage the very devotion we have demonstrated in years of study in school, and in the offices of our therapists and supervisors.

What courage is needed! What engagement with self! So throughout this book I am going to keep encouraging you to be yourself, to find your own way, to ever seek true contact, and to celebrate yourself for doing this magnificent work.

One Man's Philosophy of Therapy

The Roman poet, Virgil, directed our attention to our first "true contact." *Incipe, parve puer, risu cognoscere matrem:* "Begin, baby boy, to recognize your mother with a smile." On mother's day, a few years ago, August Wilson, author of the play, "Seven Guitars," wrote:

> "Of all human relations, that of a mother and child is the most primary, the most fundamental. It is also sometimes the most complicated and is often, given the nature of human life, an embattled relationship.
>
> Nevertheless, it is only when you encounter a world that does not contain your mother that you begin to fully comprehend the idea of loss and the huge and irrevocable absence that death occasions.
>
> Like Red Carter (a character in Seven Guitars who is offered a choice of a red or white carnation on mother's day, and says: "I need me a red flower. My mother's still living. Even as I know it got to come to the day I wear a white flower, I hope it ain't no time soon"), I knew it would come to the day, Mother's day 1983 when my brothers and sisters and I would wear a white flower for the first time. It is a rite of passage, daunting and profound, a moment of clarity in which the responsibility of your life is fully thrust into your hands. Up until that moment, whether you knew it or not, you had been, as the gospel song puts it, "living on mother's prayer."

A world without the shelter and sustenance of mother's prayer is, when you first encounter it, an alien place. It is a world in which all the known references are dismantled and the cartographers labor day and night redrawing the maps. It is a world in which you are lost, like Hansel, in what D.H. Lawrence called the "dark forest of the soul," where you battle for light and clarity while looking for sharp and good directions." (3)

In this dark forest of the soul lies my metapsychology. Some might say that this is fusion and psychological separation, a kind of attachment theory, but these terms, so necessary perhaps for us to communicate in our schools and institutes, already remove us from the dark forest of the soul. Our theories and concepts often are like the anatomical textbooks that reduce the moment of intimate love to pen and ink drawings. No textbook ever caught the moment of union with a beloved. And no metapsychology grasps the passion of life. Rather, it squeezes the life out of it. Life is not about fear and anger and attraction; it is about terror and rage and lust. If you really want to know about emotions close the textbook and spend some days with an infant or toddler. There it all is: rage, terror, shame, despair; the full expression of each. And joy and hilarity and dance and song and wet kisses and hugs and truth and power and reconciliation, I love you and (less so) I hate you and instant forgiveness and starting over and more passion and taking in and eliminating, all with joy and anguish and immediacy and finality.

My patient Arthur lost his wife to death six weeks ago. He and Pearl were on their way to a family event in Brazil, and as they exited the plane at Sao Paulo, Pearl fell to the floor. The wild scramble of helpers could do nothing to breathe the spirit of life into her exhausted body. Six hours earlier she had complained of chest discomfort but shrugged it off as chronic gall bladder trouble. Arthur suggested they go to the hospital; the trip could wait another day. No, she decided; it was probably nothing, and as they passed the hours flying south Art noticed her touching her chest now and again. She was fine she reassured him. She would eat lightly and it would pass.

Art is sixty-five years old, a vigorous and gentle man with long lives in his heritage. He stood alone in Sao Paulo that day, made arrangements, and returned to his home on Long Island where breakfast dishes were still wet in the drain. His adult daughter, returned from graduate school in Philadelphia, stood with him. Their lives would never be the same, nor those of his two sons. And many others, as well.

Art was nearly sixty when he first came for therapy, and he has used our time together as well as anyone I have ever known. He left Europe as a child, shortly before the holocaust, and began life anew with his parents and some relatives in New York. The family prospered as did his future wife's. They enjoyed a rich, full, musical and artistic life. It was a blend of European sophistication and American freshness, and they all had good times. He is a very good man, Art, a generous man. One can count on him.

One of the main themes of our work is how he overprotects others, particularly family, particularly women. His narcissistic mother was almost a caricature of self-centeredness and trained him to be at her service, while his dignified father, enjoying the culture and razzmatazz of post WW II New York, let her have her way for the most part. Art was the very model they created with all the good and all the bad. Yesterday he confided in me. "You know there is something I have been wanting to tell you but I keep forgetting. Every time I have to inform someone of Pearl's death, perhaps an acquaintance I run into, a terrible feeling comes over me: guilt. (Me: Like you let her down). Yes, like I had been remiss. It is very strong and I can't shake it. I've been meaning to tell you about it but it keeps going away."

Deep, deep inside this silver-haired gentleman, this *Paterfamlias*, a person of great accomplishments including an honorary doctorate, lives a little boy who protects his contract (and his contact!) with his mother, the psychic Versailles agreement that allowed him very little personal initiative in the creation of his life in exchange for security, for intermittent love, for release from the threat of abandonment. Many layers of experience and accomplishment covered this little boy and his coda of understanding with his mother, yet it was the energizing and organizing principle of his life. Much of that pact lived in the elaboration of its tenets in his relationship with Pearl. And now she is gone, and he is bereft. He didn't even like her much. But for years he had forsaken true contact with others for symbolic mother-contact with Pearl. Now the little boy and his coda threatens to break down, and Art is at sea.

Years before I knew what metapsychology was I knew that our relationship with mother was the most profound experience any of us would ever have. I knew it in my own experience, in that of my friends, those I saw about me. I had an intuitive sense of the fear and homage that floated around mother. I knew it in the reverence for the "Mother" of God in my church, in *mother* church, itself. The air was thick with it. Life was about mother. This was before I knew of psychology and before the power of mother was even consciously articulated to myself. My conviction persisted when, as a young student, I began to study the Freudian metapsychology. The Oedipal was intriguing to me. We all had lots of fun discovering this family drama. It was the lynchpin of theory, so much depended upon it. Naturally I blamed myself when it still seemed to me that the issue started much before, at mother's breast, and that this was true not only of psychotics and profoundly damaged individuals but of us all. Metapsychology seemed just too difficult for me to understand and so I kept my mouth shut about it.

There are many points of view in our field. How to decide which is true? Which theory should we accept? Many of us accept the theory our training institute taught us so we become as little children in bible class learning chapter and verse. Probably more frequently, we espouse the theory of our personal therapist or analyst, a transference-borne group of beliefs that carry with them our need to hold on to our analyst's wisdom. Still others search and bump into congenial theory. This is the best, but even here our tendency is to look outside ourselves for the "truth." Some of us even side step the issue and try to keep our work limited to behavior and habit change, like taking a shower with a lover fully dressed; not much contact there.

But where did all the theories come from in the first place? They came from people willing to brave the anxieties of separation by coming up with new ideas, ideas spawned to make sense of the reality each saw and heard. They did not try to fit their experience into preconceived theory. Even from the beginning, the very disciples of Freud were creating new theories, some in dramatic contradiction to his. These were not blind followers, Jung, Adler, Horney, Ferenczi, Federn, Klein, his own daughter, to mention a handful of the hundreds who rolled up their sleeves and thought profoundly and deeply regarding the phenomena they were daily engaged in. Can we not also? Can we not create our own metapsychologies?

I suspect most of us do it anyway. When the doors are shut in our consulting rooms and our personal analysts and supervisors are left outside, when the tape recorders are shut off and the pad and pencil is put down, the real work of relatedness and contact, our best work, is done. Then a metapsychology appears that is an amalgam of our training and analysis but most powerfully the manifestation of our deepest beliefs about life. Some of our distortions and crazy notions, the ones that may interfere with our hearing our patients well, may be modified by good analysis and good supervision, if we are lucky. Even so, what we learned in the school yard and in conversation with our best latency age buddy, what we concluded looking into the faces of our parents and siblings and teachers and TV characters, and most of all what we learned in our mothers' arms and in the times when even as children we "had it out with ourselves," probably supplies the greatest amount of the variance. We don't want to know this, "scientists" that we aspire to be, but it is so. And this is not necessarily bad, for it is in real contact, not theoretical expertise, that change and growth has a chance. This is a truth Linda Carrol knew, somewhere deep inside her.

Why don't we come out of the closet?

My metapsychology has to do with fusion but not only the fusion that our patients are dealing with when they come to us for relief. Equally important is the fusion that we psychotherapists live in that infiltrates our lives and loves and work to a far more profound extent than we ordinarily let ourselves know. And if we fail to courageously confront our own fusion, our work with our patients will be a tepid edition of what is possible. Yes, we must know mommy, *our* mommy, in the deepest of ways. We must understand our true contact with her, "what works; what we must leave behind." (4)

So in the rest of this chapter I will tell you a little about my understanding of psychological fusion, which informs my every encounter as a psychotherapist. I shall remind you also of our tendency as therapists to fuse with our profession and our superiors. This fusion can freeze us and block our true grasp of the other, or keep us in hiding about just what it is that we *do* do in our work. We need not be furtive. We are as good as the next person, and our not knowing this is related to the same quirk that has us second guessing ourselves in all areas of our lives: psychological fusion, pure and simple, that poor substitute for true contact. I will encourage each of us to feel deeply and live through our darkest places, unashamed.

One day, I was on my way to the 92nd St. Young Mens' and Womens' Hebrew Association in Manhattan to teach the last of four classes entitled, "Letting Go of Mother." As has happened on my walks to class the previous three weeks, an incident occurred which became the jumping off point for the discussion in the seminar. I was a little rushed and slightly frustrated when I couldn't pass two little boys about eight or nine and their mother. The three of them were blocking the street already narrowed by a big pile of garbage bags at the curb. As I struggled to get past I heard one of the boys ask his mother why he couldn't have another candy bar when he finished the one he was now enjoying. She told him he would get sick. A rejoinder by him led to his mother patiently explaining how the body's way of informing us that we are doing something not good for us is to get sick. I thought this good advice, actually, but the thing that struck me most was the attention the boys were paying to her, the contact. They were learning an important lesson, one of the seemingly infinite lessons we learn from mother, and learning it in a way that was deep and penetrating. I thought again how powerful are mother's communications to us, and for so long.

The salient reality about fusion is how pervasive it is and how deep inside us. We who know about it and use this awareness in our work and even teach of it, even we, often only realize the half of it. A colleague of mine, a psychotherapist for thirty years, told me after he read something I wrote on fusion that it was the first time that he really understood just what fusion really is. Since that time he has been seeing things in a new light, he tells me, as have his patients. A psychotherapist in her sixties who attended a class of mine told me that in all her years of therapy she hadn't really dealt with the ways she was attached to her mother, the feelings she couldn't have, the thoughts that blocked her or that she was forbidden to have, the behavior patterns that were self-defeating that had roots in the pacts she had made growing up with her mother. Amazingly frequent are the tales from therapists and patients who had been in various forms of psychotherapy and psychoanalysis for lengthy periods of time only to never have fully and deeply dealt with their enmeshment in mother. For a long time fusion-watcher like me, the signs are everywhere, all the time. Each time I teach a class I have a clipping fresh from the paper that illustrates our fusion with mother whether it is the Yankees taking their turns thanking their mothers when they won the world series to the Atlanta watchman, a suspect in the Olympic bombing, breaking down in tears in telling the world of his mother's support for him during his ordeal. They left together in embrace to return to the home he, age thirty-seven, shares with her.

We so easily attach. Thirty days ago I didn't know the fifteen persons in my four session class, but for days prior to its ending I ruminated about extending it. I worried that I would deal with the anxiety about ending by forgetting about the class altogether (as one of the students did). When I asked the class their reactions to ending, they reported all sorts of plans to maintain contact. I have received requests for individual consultations from several students. We humans do not suffer separation easily. It's all around. Observe it. Take it in.

Years ago I saw a delightful movie. I don't remember the title but it took place in a resort town in England. An Inn was bursting at the seams with guests, including the large summer staff that strained its capacity for sleeping quarters. All sorts of jerrybuilt rigs were set up. One such was a tiny attic room with a big double bed. In this bed slept two waitresses, college students most probably. With three months of living under the same roof, the young people crammed into their tiny quarters had to use significant ingenuity to arrange for the assignations which people working at a summer resort will certainly have. One of the young women began an affair with an assistant chef. Their liaisons took place late at night with the young man secreting himself into his girlfriend's bed while the roommate slept, facing away. At the end of the movie, when all the romantic bindings are being loosed, there is a scene of the roommates in the bed, the one on her side "sleeping" as usual and the heroine lying on her back without the boyfriend, crying softly, trying to stifle her tears. After a few moments the roommate turned around and said to her friend, "I know how you feel; I can't sleep without him either!" Such is the power and quickness and even quirkiness of human attachment.

When I began to write on the topic of enmeshment with mother I didn't really know whether this was any more than my unanalyzed fusion with my own mother. For more than a decade, though, the thoughts kept coming. Now as I get feedback from colleagues and patients and friends I am reassured that it is more than just my quirks. Even in the midst of studying psychoanalytic theory and being immersed in treatment from both sides of the couch, even living in the psychoanalytic milieu, vast pockets of enmeshment are ignored. What's more, our profession itself is a symptom of unanalyzed, enmeshment and unwittingly a protector of the mother-fusion pact. Daily I hear reports of it and witness its signs. And why not? Are we so different from other people? To the extent we think we are, we are enmeshed.

Metapsychology, itself, often works in the service of fusion. It is sometimes so complicated and arcane that it is impossible to use in a practical and productive way. We write more and more esoteric journal articles and we quote each other and discuss theory with each other in conferences and meetings. But how practical is it all? How much does it help? What can we bring into our consulting room that helps us make true contact with our patients? I think it often actually stands in our way. We do the good work we do in spite of it! But we suffer. We feel remiss. We feel we are not enough. We experience shame. And all of this silent madness is an indication of our own residual fusion with mother, our still trying to get the approval Barbra Streisand was searching for when after a worldwide tour of standing ovations she looks down at her 80 year-old mother in the third row and says, "Am I good enough now, mother?"

When I came up with my own metapsychology it was because, for some reason, I gave myself permission to see what I saw and to name it in a way that made sense to me. I saw that fusion was the ordinary state of affairs and not the exception. I realized that fusion was everywhere, not only in the Barbra Streisands and August Wilsons and the ordinary Joe and Jane of our everyday life. It was also in our relationship to our patients and our students and our teachers and the ordinary folks in our ordinary life. Perhaps most of all it was in our *not being aware* of the instances of fusion in ourselves and our profession and our staying fused with our mothers by being good "doctors" in distinction from the "patients." Our "concepts" were often used in the service of resistance to our own feelings. We aren't free enough to think on our own or to feel whatever it is we feel.

May I make a suggestion at this point? I ask you to keep an open mind about what I am discussing. Often we have been made so anxious about knowledge that when new ideas are presented we are uncomfortable until we can reassure ourselves, "Oh, I know that," or dismiss it with, "This is too simplistic," or remove ourselves by saying, "so and so" has already said that." Let what I am saying into you without your formulating an answer, a response, an evaluation. Let yourself "know" it. This means emptying your mind, and rather than disputing anything, listen to these notions and how your spirit responds, even if your response is unclear and unformed. If you do this, you will already be in a psychologically separating mode and will be responding to my ideas strictly from your *uniqueness* and not from the conditioning of the past. Whatever your response, whatever feelings and thoughts and bodily sensations you experience, will be yours. You will be in what I refer to as the "Wisdom Place."

Wisdom is that understanding of reality which we accrue through our own experience—in those moments when we discard all influence and see the world through our own eyes. We are always capable of moving into the place of wisdom. It can occur at any age and in any place.

"In this Wisdom place we are separate from our influences. No one lives in our brain; no script is being carried out; the chronic affects of our past experiences are muted; no obsessive distractions remove us from ourselves. We are free to see what is there, to know a feeling, an impulse, a bodily state. We are free to think, to sort out the demonic conditioning from the veridical experiences, and through this lens of who we actually are at the moment, we see what we can see. We are free at that moment of false gods: people and beliefs and behaviors that we learned could rescue us from our terror and grief. We see what is. There is no denial."(5) And each instance of wisdom is forged in the crucible of our profound love for mother. Each veridical perception is won in the struggle to see for ourselves, while terrified lest her vision be the better one.

Mother! The greatest love affair each of us will ever know. From the moment we exploded into the world outside her belly, our life has been about her. For when we woke up we woke up to her. And we woke up terrified, and she consoled us. All of our childhood and perhaps all of our life is some variation of this *main idea*. We are terrified, and she was the source of the surcease of that terror. We need to know this, especially those of us who work with people in studying their very existence. We need to know this, and we need to know it in the deepest, most emotional way, not in a textbook way. We need to experience it deeply ourselves, and we need to be open to a continuing and deepening awareness of that love and its history, its disguises and its despair, its brain-scrambling, its reparative philosophies, its life scripts, its deep unchallenged beliefs, the massive ways we humans have concocted not to know, and more important, not to FEEL. We need to know what my patient Jessica, a "generation X" social worker tells me, "I am so intimately connected with every breath she takes." Then we may live more as our true selves and be of service to those who ask us to search with them for *their* true selves.

Mom! All life has been about her, and we know just the surface, the shimmying surface of a deep pool, and we need to know the depths. These depths were created in the endless time of our visit in her womb. Current theory and some research has it that even then we were experiencing some sort of consciousness and the very beginnings of Self. And those depths filled out and magnified in the seemingly endless days and nights and weeks and years and decades of our learning of each other.

From the very beginning we were letting go, and we were distressed. We loved her with the truest of loves; we had the deep belief that we could not maintain our very lives without her; we dreaded the baleful mourning that accompanied every glimpse into our letting go of her, yet letting go was our destiny. Psychological fusion is the attempt to solve the problem of letting go by becoming enmeshed in mother. We fiercely seize the deep belief that the thoughts, feelings, perceptions, values, or behavior of our mothering person is contingent on our own thoughts, feelings, perceptions, values and behavior. Similarly, fusion refers to our tendency to regulate, consciously or unconsciously, our own thoughts, feelings, perceptions, values, and behavior with hers! *All therapeutic roads must lead to this.*

Each of us starts life terrified of life alone, painfully aware of our helplessness, and frantically depending on the mothering person to protect us. This underlying fear persists throughout life, although we tend to deny just how limited we are, the fragility of our humanity. But deep down we feel it, and unacknowledged it controls our lives. Each of us develops different psychological strategies to manage this terror and to feel *the security of enmeshment*. The different qualities of such techniques prompt us to label clusters of people together and to work toward different therapeutic techniques to deal with the "defenses" each group has developed. But regardless of the type or quality of protective mechanism, they all have at their root the attachment to mother, and growing beyond unproductive behavior will always be through the cauldron of pain and deep feeling.

And what about developmental stages, you might say. Surely the mother relationship is not the salient one in all stages, oral, anal, phallic, latency, genital and if we ride with Erikson, throughout adulthood, early, middle and late. Surely it is, I answer. The battle is joined at the very beginning and continues throughout all the following stages; the mother child relationship is key, both influencing and being influenced by the varying developmental challenges that our physiology and spirit demand of us. Nor do we ever "complete" any stage. Each stage is informed by the earlier ones that spice it up a bit. If it spices too much we have a "childish" person, if too little, we have an old man before his time. It is our bent to fuse, to stay enmeshed as a protection, whatever form this enmeshment takes, whether it is a form of "staying like" mother or her surrogate or "hating her."

But at the same time each of us has within a fierce spirit that is struggling to show itself, to birth its own uniqueness. It has been said that all of life is a recovery from childhood, a struggle to overcome a sort of post-hypnotic suggestion. My understanding is that all of life is a dialectic between that part of us which wants to stay enmeshed and that part of us, our spirit, that wants to express the once in the history of the universe person that each of us is.

Transcendence

I use the word "spirit" to refer to the life energy that is in each of us and prompts all living things to grow. This principle is outside conscious control and transcends what we can accomplish by our wills. This is why I like the term Transcendent. It is called many things by many people: God, Tao; the Jewish tradition consider it so sacred that the very mentioning of its name is forbidden. Recently I read a book by the Japanese novelist and philosopher Hiroyuki Itsuki. The title is "Tariki" which refers to this energy as *Other Power.*

> "Tariki is one of the most important concepts in Japanese Buddhism, one which first emerged during a period of tremendous upheaval and suffering in Japan, a time that called into question humanity's efforts to control its destiny. Tariki stands in contrast to 'Self-Power,' or Jirike. Since its beginnings in India, Buddhism has taught a long and arduous path of practice to reach enlightenment. This personal effort made to achieve enlightenment is a manifestation of Self-Power. Tariki, on the other hand, is the recognition of the great, all-encompassing power of the Other—in this case, the Buddha and his ability to enlighten us—and the simultaneous recognition of the individual's utter powerlessness in the face of the realities of the human condition. It is, in my opinion, a more realistic, more mature, and more quintessentially modern philosophy than Self-Power, and it is a philosophy that can be a great source of strength to live in our world today." (6)

This seems similar to the concept of Higher Power employed with incomparable success by the 12 Step programs. Nor is it at odds with the observation and experiences of science. Einstein spoke of it. In fact, all genius level scientists are humble in confrontation with this power. David Winnicott once wrote, "let down your tap root to the centre of your soul; suck up the sap from the infinite source of your unconscious and be evergreen."

It seems to be an easier notion in some "primitive cultures." Chief Seattle's tribe had a simple prayer: " May all I do think and feel today be consistent with you, God within me, God around me, Maker of the trees." In the European Christian tradition things are not so clear. This life energy is what the early Christian thinkers referred to as *Magnum Mysterium*, the great mystery.

It sure is a mystery to me. We don't know where we came from; we don't know where we are going; we don't know the purpose of existence. Neurosis aside, we all suffer unspeakable agony, as I saw on the face of my wife as she learned of her father's death. She was bereft, suffering anguish beyond words. I felt an agony of my own, witnessing her suffering and being unable to spare her. As the Buddhists remind us, we are born crying, we live in mystery, we grow old, we get sick and we die. That we can count on. It seems unlikely that science will ever be of much help here. It seems to be the human condition. We humans have to live in this magnum mysterium, follow our spirits and gamely go on. For the most part we do, which is the essence of our greatness. It is the God within us. Humankind has from the beginning known of this Transcendent power even if its workings have been sometimes mystifying to us. And in all the spiritual literature the battle has been drawn between our self-centered fusion and our intrinsic push to grow. If you look closely you will see, from our earliest teachings, the awareness that psychological separation is key to the freeing of the human spirit. "Whoever loves father or mother more than me is not worthy of me" (Mt. 10:37), for example.

This struggle is often wild and passionate, the spirit fighting for its life, gasping for air, and the forces of fusion, demonic in intensity and relentless, always on the ready to subvert and sabotage new life. *Good psychotherapy is the rare instrument that takes the side of spirit in that struggle.* The person who seeks out psychotherapy is brave, indeed. And so is his therapist. Each must face the music of the layers of emotions that comprise us, although we may present a pleasant melody to most audiences. One wants to be a good patient; one wants to appear as a competent therapist. Both are trying to please their mothers. Later, in chapter five, on we will speak of the nature of psychological and spiritual change, and I will share with you my understanding of the process and some of the aspects of our contact with patients that are healing. But one point is so important to everything that I want to speak of it early on. And that is *affect, for if we avoid affect, no contact is ever possible* and psychotherapy becomes a mere intellectual exercise. Emotions! We are all terrified of them; they are so unpredictable and uncontrollable. And it is true that emotions are uncontrollable, but why control them anyway. They are our flesh and blood, the charm and color of life, the source of our most important information about ourselves and the world. But they are terrifying to us, others, our parents. We have been seriously constricted about their expression. The injunction to control even the experience of our emotions is one of the chief mechanisms which fosters fusion. Without the possibility to at least experience our emotions we can never be free, be ourselves, can never help our patients take a foray into the truths and terrors and beauties of their spirit. Emotion is the language of the spirit. Living in emotions in psychotherapy and everywhere is a crucial element of my personal theory.

Living In Emotions

Let me start by examining what do we do with a "bad" affect that won't go away even after one has experienced, studied, and understood it? This is part of a larger discussion of management of affects in general. We can divide this problem into two parts. One refers to the psychic mechanisms, mostly unconscious, which deny, bury, transform, reverse or perform all manner of cognitive and affective mayhem in the service of *not feeling* the affect and not knowing the content, object, aim or whatever of the impulse underlying the affect. So we don't want to know our urges, our emotions, and the cast of characters involved in them. We might refer to these hijinks as intrapsychic, or psychological mechanisms of defense.

Second, is the question of "management" of these affects once they do break into conscious awareness. This breaking into consciousness can be a friendly intrusion in the sense that a person wants to know his affective experience, cherish it, and understand its deep epistemological value, even if it rattles him a little at first. If we know what we feel we are forced to take a good look around us, and we are going to learn a lot. Or perhaps the person is new to the *Wisdom Path* but is willing to let happen what needs to happen to continue on that path. She may be in the process of allowing awareness of more affect than she ordinarily does, though this may be new and a little disorienting to her at first. Finally, there are those who do not welcome more affect, but the intrapsychic mechanisms of defense fail them, and they feel more than they want or believe they can tolerate.

What "management of affect" strategies are available to us? Of course we can use drugs and knock out most of the feeling. Some use personally concocted remedies such as alcohol, food, sex, work, danger, wherein the remedy for the affect is in something external and non-human (I use the word affect rather than pain because many folks dampen positive affects, too. You can be afraid of happiness if you come from a home where security was found in fused suffering).

Then there are the *inter*-psychic life strategies designed to manage affect. A dependent relationship, an "enabling" one, a loving mutual relationship, a good friendship. With varying degrees of violation of integrity, we use others to make us feel better. We can participate in groups (including professional psychotherapy organizations), the faithful membership in which can give us the experience of mother-pleasure. All of the above are some form of arranging to have Mommy kiss our "boo-boos." I don't mean this as criticism. Life is hard. We all need help, and we all need surcease.

But what do we do when we are on our own? We are off by ourselves (like we all experienced lying in the crib some years ago, upset, parents fast asleep, with no phone nearby nor bartender nor psychotherapist to talk to) and cannot or *choose* not to use whatever remedies may be available to us even if they are nearby? We have to handle this by ourselves. What do we do?

Some with a spiritual bent advise prayer and meditation. These techniques may use slogans, aphorisms, especially those connected to a parental surrogate. When used in a spiritual quest they are quite wonderful. When used primarily with the intention of ridding ourselves of pain they fall into the category of the nostrums described above. I am not critical of this at all. Life *is* tough.

But suppose you decide not to "get rid" of the affect. What is left after you have experienced, studied and understood the affect, and you are still suffering? Well, you can keep on feeling it for starters. David Reynolds (7), the American standard bearer for a type of therapy created by the Japanese physician, Shoma Morita (8), taught that since we have no control over our emotions we might as well go about our business, because we always have control over that. The feelings will pass in time as emotions do. Give up any attempt to control them; don't even pay them much heed. When a patient has experienced, studied and "understood" an emotion and the affect still lingers, sometimes powerfully, I do the following. I encourage the patient to stay fully with the feeling, to accept it, and to *accept himself having this feeling*. I deal with all the self-critical ideation he generates as a result of his inability to "change" the feeling. If he is to be critical I encourage him to be critical of me since I haven't helped him not to feel this way. (Later he will learn, hopefully, that criticism, like resentment, is an all-or-nothing proposition. If she is to fully, *radically* accept herself she will have to forgive and accept all others, but that truth is for later). I point out to her that if she ceases doing *anything* to "get rid" of the affect, at the very least it will pass on its own as feelings do, like a river running to the sea. The feeling might actually "burn itself out" as affect does when deeply experienced, so perhaps she will be finally healed of it. Or, deeply experiencing the feeling and not "offing" it will give us clues to feelings and ideas, perhaps deep beliefs, in deeper nooks and crannies of her psyche. Encouraging her to merely observe, to gently witness her state, can temper her fear. I reassure her that I, too, have suffered greatly and have come through it stronger and happier. We make contact with each other.

Her watching herself withstand the pain of affects that she believed would destroy her enables her to see that she can survive. She develops a certain psychic robustness. At best she will know a deepening of her relationship with *herself*. She will learn at ever deepening levels that she can be alone with herself and even love herself. No matter what life dishes out, she knows she will be OK, and she will be getting a better friend, herself, throughout this journey. She will have made true contact with herself. At the same time patients report that when they allow themselves to feel feelings, even though they sometimes feel discouraged, or upset that they are upset, their interactions with others reach new possibilities. They find themselves doing things in relating to others that they have never done before. They experience a remarkable increase in *contact* with other persons.

I apply this technique to myself. Recently, I have been feeling discomfort at the end of the weekly psychotherapy group I lead. I have been studying the problem and consulting with colleagues, and what I determined is a that a particular patient, the recently widowed Art, has been behaving in a way that inhibits the spontaneous flow of the other patients. He is a distinguished looking, benevolent man who people tend to look toward for approval. He precludes any attack on himself by protecting others from "attacks." These "attacks" are generally merely attempts to understand the inner processes of an individual or to foster the progressive flow of communication and emotional contact. When someone speaks, he "conditions" them by nodding his head and smiling. No one calls him on this, and so great is their gratification that when I do, no one agrees, and this stirs up discomfort in me. The death of his wife and some business reverses have shaken him, but he does not bring these up in group. I have worked with Art for a long time, but I am just now noticing a certain deviousness in him that I hadn't been aware of, and I am horrified.

Recently two new members joined the group. They are very interactive and have stirred things up considerably. Art has reacted with depression, lack of participation, denial of interpretations and absence. After a recent group I was very upset. I decided to stay with these feelings and not use one of the many ways I have of denying, minimizing, even "resolving" painful affects. I spent the better part of the next day steeped in the feeling, an emotion that returned every time I thought of the previous night's group and of Art. Finally, I got it. The feeling was shame. When I realized this I got some release of the "bad" feeling and obsession for the remainder of the day. That night, before going to sleep, the obsession and its accompanying dark feeling returned. My sleep was fitful and I woke to the same disquiet; it lingered the rest of the day. I was determined not to talk my way out of it, not to use any of the psychic magic potions that I have to alter affect; I promised myself not to act out. This time I was going to stay the course. During the day I experienced rage. "How could he do this to me? And after all I have done for him! What is the matter with that group that they let him get away with this? To hell with it, maybe I'll stop doing group therapy altogether!"

I knew I was feeling overly responsible for what happened in the group, an old problem for me. I felt in a trap. If I confront him with his behavior, no one will support me, and he will defeat me by his withdrawal, maybe even leave group. If I don't, the group is dead and I am not helping anyone at all, the worst of all possibilities. Then it dawned on me. I was responding to this situation not merely with my old codependent dynamics of taking responsibility for the affect of others as I had learned growing up with my own mother. I was also responding to Art not "as if" he were my mother but in a deeper and more primitive way. I was responding to him *as* my mother. It wasn't similar to the past; it *was* the past. It was a kind of "psychotic" countertransference in its intensity.

I was astounded. I had lost contact with Art and with myself and wound up in an isolated contact with the mother I could never please, never influence! This deep realization rang so true to me and explained the intensity of the affect. Immediately the painful affect left! In thinking about it there were certain circumstances in Art's life that contributed to my switching over into this unreal transference. I had begun to experience him as "evil," and the pain was as severe as when I discovered some aspects of my mother I considered evil. But now that it was conscious I could forgive him as I had her and get about the business of helping all of us experience and communicate our feelings to each other.

My staying with my feelings those two days enabled me to experience a very deep pre-verbal affect, and release it. Another step was taken on my own lifetime journey of psychological separation. As I think about the situation with Art and the group now I feel a sense of peace and an eagerness to lovingly resume our work together. I am no longer afraid. Surely, I am not always so brave. Often I use all the ways I know to get myself to feel better. But the times I do explore this way enrich me and often change me profoundly—much more so than when I approach the problem by demanding that I "understand."

In the midst of the cacophony of influences, inner and outer, mother saying this, father saying that, identifying with mother, protecting mother from father, and so forth, there is also the voice of *spirit,* the psychologically separating self that is trying to be heard amidst the din. Listen to it, for it is you, the unique once in the history of the universe person that you are. You owe it to the world to show your spirit. Feel the knot of terror in your stomach; be aware of the tears behind your eyes, bear the relentless obsessing and criticism. And do not act from them. *You do not have to!* Rather, act from spirit, from *you!* In the midst of all the racket within, you are free. Find that freedom, fight for it. It is your birthright, your gift to all humankind. You are always free to select spirit voice over all other influences. This, incidentally, is why radical self-acceptance is so important (more about this in chapter five). Radical self-acceptance is the calisthenics for the spirit. It strengthens the spirit, so when you must make the choice among all the voices, it will be clear. You will always know when you go with the spirit voice because you never have regrets.

From our earliest moments, and certainly from our earliest moments of consciousness, we have been engaged in mortal combat between that part of us that wants to stay fused with the safety and warmth and promised eternity of the mothering one, and that part of us, our spirit, that wants to break out and away from the fusion, to explore the world, to brave the unknown, to see with our own eyes. That dialectic, passion for life versus the demons of stasis, with which each of us has been engaged since birth continues now, and the battle is often fierce! We are all filled with rage and terror and a terrible grieving for what we've lost and are losing, and we're all constantly building or maintaining a thrown together structure to keep these feelings in check.

My patient Art, when grieving for Pearl, said to me, "I feel that's one less person I have to be alive for."

> Me: "Who else?"
> "My mother was one; my wife was one."
> Me: "Wow! Now you're going to have it out with yourself...if there's no one else to be alive for, can you be alive for yourself?"

Our work is to help ourselves and others know that it is all right to *feel* things deeply—not necessarily to express them, but to *experience* them, to know deeply, to receive the deep beliefs that come with this experiencing, to make *contact* with others, to make room for our spirits to resume their natural movement toward true self. As we grow in radical self acceptance, each of us, patient and therapist, will know that it is all right to be alive, unencumbered, free. To be a courageous psychotherapist you have to discover and nurture your own unique spirit. Then that spirit forages in the dark forest of the soul of your patient, looking for his spirit. And when your spirit discovers his, in true contact, he is alive again.

Summary

1. There is miraculous work done by psychotherapists all over the world. Most of this great work is done by the "ordinary" professional, the "grunt in the trenches," not the "stars" in the psychoanalytic think tanks and great universities who often write esoteric books and articles, mostly for themselves. The ordinary psychotherapist tends to feel intimidated by these weighty tomes.

2. Each therapist does her work out of who she is, the amalgam of training and personal psychotherapy, but mostly her own unique "take" on the world which she has developed out of her own personality and experience. But she tends to do her work furtively, trying to be acceptable to the "authorities" of her profession.

3. I encourage each therapist to "come out of the closet," and articulate, at least to herself, exactly what she believes about life and the nature of psychological struggle. Most important, I hope she would see clearly just what about her contact with her patients is helpful.

4. I offer my own views on this, not to entice others to agree with me, but rather to encourage each reader to focus on her own. A central conviction of mine is that we are all more fused with our family of origin than we acknowledge, typically mostly with mother, and that this fusion interferes with our uniqueness and our freedom.

5. It is the intensity of our relationship with mother and the duress of the prospect of separating from her that leads often to psychological

fusion as a solution to that terror. Psychological fusion is having our thoughts, emotions, beliefs and behaviors so intertwined with another (mostly mother or a surrogate) that it is not clear just who is doing the acting.

6. The opposite of this security of enmeshment is the accomplishment of "the wisdom place." This is when our connection to our forebears is disentangled sufficiently so that we are able to see the world through our own eyes and think our own thoughts and feel our own feelings.

7. It is our bent to be fused, our natural tendency as humans. At the same time we have a force inside us, an instance of life energy I call spirit. This spirit fights against this fusion and pushes toward wisdom, just as a toddler struggles to stand and walk. This force is internal yet part of the greater power of life, something transcendent, however you define it. Winnicott said, "let down your tap root to the centre of your soul; suck up the sap from the infinite source of your unconscious and be Evergreen."

8. All life is a dialectic between the "demons" of fusion which wants us fused and the passion of the spirit which claws for freedom. *Good psychotherapy is the rare instrument that sides with spirit in that struggle.*

9. Emotions are the language of the spirit. We must learn to live in them, to not be afraid. Essential to growth is the emerging capacity to tolerate affect, accepting all feelings and your very self in the process.

Notes

(1) Egan T. N.Y. Times Op-Ed page (9/16/93)
(2) Schachtel, E. *Metamorphosis* (New York: Basic Books, 1959)
(3) Wilson, A. Op-Ed page *N.Y. Times*, May 12, 1996
(4) McMahon, J. *Letting Go of Mother.* (New York / Mahwah, N.J.: Paulist Press, 1996)

(5) _____ *The Price of Wisdom.* (New York: Crossroad Press, 1996)

(6) Itsuki, Hiroyuki. *Tariki.* (Tokyo: Kodanshka Ltd: 2001) p.xvii

(7) Reynolds, D. *The Quiet Therapies: Japanese Pathways to Personal Growth.* (Honolulu: Hawaii, 1980)

(8) Morita, S. *Shinkeishitsu No Hontai To Ryoho [Nature of Neurosis and Its Therapy].* (Tokyo: Hakuyosha, 1983)

2

Is There Such a Thing as Psychopathology?

Recently John Bayley wrote in his touching story of life with his famous wife, novelist Iris Murdoch, as she was engulfed in the mists of Alzheimer's disease, "every 'ordinary' person is, in fact, extraordinary, often grotesquely so, and in every sort of way." (1) In the 1970's I read an interview with Henry Miller in which he was asked to assess his impact on the world of literature. He responded that he never thought about that. All people, he believed, were pretty much the same, the greatest not so different from the least. "To be human, truly human, that is quite enough for me." And, of course, the great American psychiatrist Harry Stack Sullivan, working in the bowels of the mental hospitals of the 1940's and 1950's treating the most difficult and largely unmedicated patients, offered his famous teaching: "We are all more human than otherwise."

When I was a kid I learned to read a primer which was, in a sense, a window to the world. And it was a perfect world, with a perfect Jane and a perfect Dick and a perfect Mom and Dad and a perfect Policeman and Fireman and Mailman and a perfect Dog, Spot.

All alone (I thought), I considered how different I was from all those perfect people that I read about in my primer.

I've come to know that most, if not all, of my classmates were having the same experience. And yet there we sat, all thirty of us, feeling alone and isolated, and under no circumstances were we to communicate our feelings to another. And so we all remained isolated from each other throughout life.

When some of us showed up at the door of a Mental Health practitioner hoping to get some relief, the lie was continued and our worst fears were reaffirmed; we, indeed, were different from others—especially from the perfect Doctors.

Some knew about this and kept their pain to themselves, groping quietly for consolation, in bodies or substances, or fantasies or whatever.

All of us—doctors, patients, and those on the lam—remain alone and isolated, with little contact. How sad.

How worried people are about the state of their mental health! The state of one's psyche is worried about the way the state of one's soul used to be, I suspect, before the Freudian revolution. In the temples of the priests of psychopathology and mental health, certain diagnostic categories are definitely frowned upon. This seems to change from generation to generation, even in the limited time period we have had to observe the replacement of sin by "psychopathology."

An illustration: although from its very beginning women were powerful participants in the creation of the psychoanalytic movement, psychoanalysis was basically created by men, Victorian men. I believe we humans tend to label pathological that which is different from ourselves. That which is different from ourselves is often frightening. That which is frightening we often disapprove of. So these conquistadors of the soul were confronted with women, and there was a great focus on the "illness" of Hysteria. Hysteria, as technically defined in those days, was not restricted to women, but the fact that its name comes from the Greek word for womb tells you whom they were talking about.

There were just a few categories of "pathology" acceptable at that time. Acceptable were those personalities that could be explained by the theory and which also responded to the techniques of treatment that classical psychoanalysis provided.

As time passed pessimism developed due to the erratic results of the technique. The theory was changed somewhat, and now the "pathology" we had to deal with was a new set of personalities, the "character disorders." Over the years we had difficulty with these blokes as well. We were rescued from this dilemma by the advent of the "borderlines" who themselves proved particularly bothersome because once again they would not respond to what we had to offer. Currently we are absorbed with the "narcissists," a particular brand of borderline. From the beginning, "psychotics" have been excluded as well as the "perversions" who psychotherapists seem to have particular disdain for.

From the beginning of modern dynamic psychology there has been a subtle, but real, judgmental quality to the diagnosis of "psychopathology." We humans have a very strong tendency to judge and evaluate. At the bottom of all of this judgment, I suspect, is the belief that we ourselves are not good enough, and so we search for some relief from this deep, painful belief by making comparisons. We are always compared, aren't we? From the beginning we are assigned size places, alphabetical order, IQ scores, achievements of one sort or another. Rarely do we hear, especially as children, "I love you just the way you are." If you think mental health practitioners are above this sort of thing, you are wrong. If anything we are worse. We come into this profession obsessed with our own mental functioning as well as that of others. Our need to "cure" comes profoundly from our own experience and needs. All the years of study and all the degrees on the wall speak of decades of surviving comparison, rising to the top of a hierarchical structure that promised that when we had completed the course we were special, above the others. One need not succumb to this indoctrination, but ever since Adam and Eve's slip up it is difficult to avoid doing so.

The main problem I have with the concept of diagnosis and psychopathology is that it fits so neatly into our ever-ready tendency toward classifying each other. This classification isolates us from true contact. When we evaluate another human being and classify her (forget, for the moment, the inconsistency of these evaluations by differing clinicians), we kid ourselves that we really know who she is, how she functions, how all this came about, and just what needs to be done to make her OK. And we don't. What's more, we do not think in terms of what this particular organization of traits may be accomplishing for her at the present. Our overall attitude toward what we term "psychopathology" is that it is bad, though it would never be expressed so baldly. If the patient also thinks this, perhaps only because society has indoctrinated him, we certainly will reinforce this. Unwittingly, we often encourage the problem, and sometimes make it worse. Human beings tend to become what we are told we are. If we are told we are damaged goods we will believe this. The very structure of the doctor-patient relationship is, in this sense, encouraging of the "illness."

The truth is that when a person experiences what he considers to be a problem in living and consults one who is bold enough to present herself as an expert in these matters, what needs to be accomplished is a gently shared experience of loving kindness. The notion of "pathology" works against this. It is based on a model of sickness and illness, which is not helpful in the psychological and spiritual realms. It ignores the constant quest toward health which, though sometimes hidden, resonates in each of us. It blinds us to what should be a humble and non-judgmental inquiry into the nature and meaning of the seeking person's experience. Sometimes our white coats blind us to where we all have come from.

In his book, The Immense Journey (2), a long-time hero of mine, naturalist and poet Loren Eisely, reminds us of our roots.

> "I have long been an admirer of the octopus. The cephalopods are very old, and they have slipped, protean, through many shapes. They are the wisest of the mollusks, and

I have always felt it to be just as well for us that they never came ashore, but there are other things that have.

There is no need to be frightened. It is true some of the creatures are odd, but I find the situation rather heartening than otherwise. It gives one a feeling of confidence to see nature still busy with experiments, still dynamic, and not through nor satisfied because a Devonian fish managed to end as a two-legged character with a straw hat. There are other things brewing and growing in the oceanic vat. It pays to know there is just as much future as there is past. The only thing that doesn't pay is to be sure of man's own part in it.

There are things down there still coming ashore. Never make the mistake of thinking life is now adjusted for eternity. It gets into your head—the certainty, I mean—the human certainty, and then you miss it all: the things on the tide flats and what they mean, and why, as my wife says, 'they ought to be watched.'" (pp. 47-48)

Eisely goes on to describe the beginning. "It began as such things always begin—in the ooze of unnoticed swamps, in the darkness of eclipsed moons. It began with a strangled gasping for air…The pond was a place of reek and corruption, of fetid smells and oxygen-starved fish breathing through laboring gills" (pp. 49-50). In this environment, Eisely tells us, "The human brain began."

All fish life adapted to these conditions, hiding from the intense heat of the day, burrowing in the primordial ooze of the bottom to escape the frigid air of the night. All were in search of oxygen and the "best adapted" found it, and were the most comfortable. There was also in these waters a creature, the Snout, who was failing at getting oxygen in this highly competitive place. Yet, he had a strange attribute. His lust for air, worsened by its increasing scarceness, led, over an estimated 300 million years, to his developing a strange capacity, an awkward, bumbling but real ability to walk! As each of the ponds he struggled to live in got smaller and dried out he found himself able to hobble to the next one, ingesting oxygen along the way. He was ugly and grotesque, but he was alive.

> "There was something fermenting in the brain of the Snout. He was no longer entirely a fish. The ooze had marked him. It takes a swamp-and-tide-flat zoologist to tell you about life; it is in this domain that the living suffer great extremes, it is here that the water-failure, driven to desperation, make starts in a new element. It is here that strange compromises are made and new senses are born. The Snout was no exception. Though he breathed and walked primarily in order to stay in the water, he was coming ashore.
>
> He was not really a successful fish except that he was managing to stay alive in a noisome, uncomfortable, oxygen-starved environment. In fact the time was coming when the last of his kind, harried by more ferocious and speedier fishes, would slip off the edge of the continental shelf, to seek safety in the sunless abysses of the deep sea. But the Snout was a fresh water Crossopterygian, to give him his true name, and cumbersome and plodding though he was, something had happened back of his eyes. The ooze had gotten in its work.
>
> It is interesting to consider what sort of creatures we, the remote descendants of the Snout, might be except for that green quagmire out of which he came. Mammalian insects perhaps we should have been—solid-brained, our neurones wired for mechanical responses, our lives running out with the perfection of beautiful intricate, and mindless clocks. More likely we should never have existed at all. It was the Snout and the ooze that did it. Perhaps there also, among rotting fish heads and blue, night-burning bog lights, moved the eternal mystery, the careful finger of God. The increase was not much. It was two bubbles, two thin-walled little balloons at the end of the Snout's small brain. The cerebral hemispheres had appeared." (pp. 51-52)

It is a human liability, I think, to believe that our time on the planet, this moment, is it. It is as though one could have interrupted a moment on the 100 million year journey of the Snout and said, "this is it!" This is the way it is. This is the truth. So, too, we are in the midst of our own 100 million year journey, and this is just a moment. When we label and diagnose each other with such certainty, we forget this. We even forget how much our labels and categories have changed, even in the past 100 years.

Is there such a thing as psychopathology? I'm not so sure. At the very least we must be vigilant lest we lose the compassion and contact that "diagnosing" others can lead to. Surely some of our brothers and sisters suffer from severe biological problems that manifest themselves in psychotic behaviors. This is not truly "psycho" pathology. But even among those folks, keen contact-observation often reveals heroic examples of the struggle between spirit and demons that each human must engage in. The struggle to rescue our spirits from the control of our earliest caretakers is indeed universal; there are no exceptions. That struggle often leads to strange looking solutions—some of these some call psychopathology—but the strangest is nothing more than the heroic struggle of a fellow human being to wrest herself from the bonds of fusion with mother, and it needs to be respected as that. The snout probably would have been assigned an ominous diagnosis in the case conferences of our hospitals and universities. Who knows where other "strange" people may be leading us on our evolutionary journey? Regardless, we are all capable of everything, and nothing anyone does is not in the behavioral repertoire of each of us, however remote the likelihood of its appearance. Denying this is trouble. True knowledge of each other does not come from objective categorizing. The only way to truly know another is in related emotional contact. And if our scientific hubris blinds us to this we will have missed by a mile.

But what about suffering? Do we not suffer? And what about destructive behavior—to ourselves and to others? Do we not hurt each other? And aren't there "developmental" steps along the way that most humans seem to take, and isn't significant failure to take these steps "sick"?

As far as I can determine, "Mental Health" is being able to do what you want to do without hurting yourself or anyone else. This involves certain basic capabilities. You need to know what you want. More basic than this you must be able to "want" at all. (We will discuss this in detail in chapter five.) Then you must be able to act, to take efficacious steps toward achieving for yourself that which you have let yourself know that you want. Then you must be aware of the consequences of the acts. You must notice them, and later on you must be able to anticipate those consequences prior to your actions. These capacities are what we psychologists refer to as ego functions: perception, cognition, volition, affect, memory, judgment, in short, the ability to access the prompting of our instinctual and volitional life, understand the nature of the world adequately, and impact upon that world to get our needs met.

As we move through life and attempt to accomplish this, we must constantly deal with an enormous inertia, a paradoxical tendency toward stasis. Any act that is away from the familiar is fraught with anxiety (the fear of danger long past). As we have seen, this stasis that opposes the life urge, spirit, is based on unconscious ideas formulated by a person under duress. This duress consists of the ordinary challenges of the developmental period the individual is in. There may be stresses that lead to some variation of the following "deep beliefs": I am not all right, and I will not get the approval of the persons upon whom my survival depends and, consequently, I am in mortal jeopardy.

The conceptual and behavioral elaborations of these beliefs, theorists refer to as character structure. As adults we are constantly looking for people and situations in which to fashion an adult-looking version of the old drama. As I mentioned before, it is clear to me that it is not impulse and defense that are the key issues, but rather how the drama around impulse and defense affected the separation versus fusion struggle. These separation issues pervade our lives, and it is wise to think of them just that way, as separation issues, rather than as psychopathology.

Does this mean that there is no point in studying how we work psychologically, both intrapsychically and behaviorally? The past hundred years have taught us a great deal about how we work psychologically. It is how we use this information or hypotheses that can be a problem. For what we have learned is really a drop in the bucket. In our anxious hubris we psychotherapists tend to lose sight of this. Our need to control and change things can lead to a loss of perspective. Worst of all is a loss of humility in our relatedness with those who consult us and that loss of humility inevitably mutes true contact.

Take, for example, a "hot" diagnosis of the day, narcissism. Colloquially, a narcissist is one who is grandly self-centered. Clinically, it has been rightly observed that such self-centeredness stems from experiences that have seriously undermined his self-concept so that he actually feels subhuman. The self-centered braggart is so terrified that he is worth so little that there is some question in his mind about whether he is worthy of existing at all. Typically, he manifests unpleasant characteristics. While he can be charming and interesting in the short term, his lack of caring and true interest in others soon becomes apparent. He often looks cocky, and one would never dream that his sense of autonomy is so shaky that any comment about him is seen as a deathly threat. A criticism? Horrors! Criticism devastates the narcissistic person because his terror demands he be perfect to be minimally acceptable. He must be perfect in every way at all times and to all people and this perfection must be publicly acknowledged or at least asserted. (By the way such a person claims "no problems" with mother or the mother surrogate, often the father in the case of narcissistic women. Such a parent is "perfect" just as everything associated with the narcissist is perfect, perfect friend of the moment, perfect school attended, perfect car driven, etc.) His deep beliefs about his lack of worth, his fragile autonomy, his need to be perfect to be acceptable, the mortal danger to him if he is not constantly and publicly reassured as to his magnificence (minimal adequacy to him) keeps him vigilant and seriously interferes with his ability to relate or even to maintain a sustained interest in an activity if it no longer contributes to self-centered enhancement.

Even in the simplest of human graces one sees the invasion of this painful personality organization. Such a person, for example, while always demanding acknowledgment from others, finds it absolutely impossible to thank anyone directly. This would imply that he owes something to another, a threat to his autonomy, and that perhaps the other person had some positive traits, a threat to his own self-worth. The successes or capabilities of others cause him pain. He is riddled with envy. Naturally, he cannot admit he has made a mistake. If it is suggested that he erred he will not rest until he has extracted an acquiescence of some sort from his "accuser" that he, in fact, has not. Everything that happens is seen in the context of his own self-worth. Gratitude is impossible; it is experienced as self-depleting. Generosity is gnarled. If a generous act is performed or he gives a gift, it is stored away in memory awaiting that moment when it will be repaid. If it is not repaid up to the standards of the narcissistic person, there will be boiling resentment. While generosity and gratitude are not easily accessible to him, envy and resentment and even hate are. The result is vast self-conscious suffering and little room for love or true contact. It is very sad.

Is this not psychopathology? I think it is a common manifestation of the human condition, if a little extreme. After all, why would all the spiritual traditions over the past five thousand years rail against such behavior? If it is so pathological, how come so many of us have it, or some aspect of it, to the extent that it has been the preoccupation of literature for our entire recorded history! A problem? Certainly. Psychopathology? I'm not so sure.

In good psychotherapy, diagnosis is replaced by the mutual search and examination of the discrepancy between one's goals and one's behavior. What characterizes effective, human psychotherapy is the focus on the patient and the respectful attempt at experiencing the patient by the therapist, at making contact. While careful to avoid too much focus on self the therapist must take pains to make it clear that he feels in no way superior to the patient. To resist acting superior to the patient he, of course, must feel in no way superior to the patient. To accomplish this the therapist needs to get a handle on his own shame, and on his own narcissism. The ultimate cure for shame comes in the realization that we are all the same, that one is not so different from the other, that we are all flawed. Each patient I have known these past thirty years has taught me much. Psychotherapy can work, unwittingly, against this healing if the therapist uses his role to medicate his own narcissistic problem by feeling superior to the patient.

The Buddhists consider those personality characteristics we westerners call pathological as "hindrances" to the full development of the spirit. If we keep a gentle eye on these hindrances, both of our patients and ourselves, psychotherapy can be extraordinarily helpful. But diagnosis, (labeling, name-calling) is subtly assaultive. For one thing it breaks contact. All our lives we are told that who we are is not all right, should not be accepted, should not be let to unfold, that there is something wrong with the way we are. Diagnosis and the concept of psychopathology reinforce this. Psychotherapy has this same danger because inherent in it is the lie that the patient is broken and needs to be fixed, and that the doctor is OK. Both diagnosis and the ethic of therapeutic goals contribute to the danger of increasing the already enormous load of shame that each of us carries. In this sense the treatment itself carries the danger of being anti-therapeutic. This inherent reinforcing of the person's pain must be overcome at the outset. Different types of hindrances (character traits, personality organizations, "symptoms") may be helped by specific ways of intervening, but at the moment of the "intervention" the therapist must be engaged with a fellow human being whom he deeply believes is his equal in every way. He must be in contact. Without this contact, though we may be brilliant in our understanding, we shall fail in our purpose.

Each of us has difficulties in living. Because of the faultedness of our development, each of us has a blockage in our perceptions of the world around us. The mother of an extremely intelligent 28 year-old patient of mine, for example, hangs up on her when she discovers that her daughter had received her prior call, but did not return it the same day. "You live alone," she complained. "How do I know you haven't died?" The daughter, riddled with guilt-born fusion, calls back and tries to explain. The father of a 29-year-old man inveighs to his son who wants to move to a different state: "I'd like you to stay in Chicago, but if you must go." Both of these young adults are contaminated in their quest for independent lives by parents who will not let go, and even worse, continually throw up psychological roadblocks, double binding messages which scramble the minds of their children.

Psychological separation is such a difficult task, and when it is fought covertly by either party, it is even more difficult. Sometimes it is the adult "child" who binds his parents and prompts them to feel guilty for encouraging appropriate separation. More typically, it is the interaction of both that keeps fusion alive. Either could break out at any time, for psychological separation is essentially the responsibility of each of us, on our own. But if an adult "child" is being sabotaged by a parent, this is probably a pattern that goes back to the child's earliest years (and the parents', as well!). The child was probably raised in an ambience of fusion, marked by confused communication, binding messages that scramble the child's thinking and affect. In the air, constantly, was some variation of these messages:

1. You owe me.

2. You cannot make it without me. (and/or)

3. I will fall apart if you leave me.

We learn what is possible in communication by the kinds of communication that we were taught. Maureen's mother, for example, never responded to her daughter's communications regarding positive feelings or events in Maureen's life. She either halfheartedly replied, "that's nice, dear" or changed the subject to some narcissistic reference of her own. Maureen learned to always have gloomy things to tell her mother, and by extension, all others in her life. Intimacy was only allowed around pessimistic topics. To have contact, one must be suffering. To feel happy, one would be alone.

Erroneous perception of the world, faulty thinking, and learned constraints about what is possible in living result in emotions that are appropriate to the world we knew, not the world that is. But is this truly "pathological"? Is it "abnormal"? Only in the sense that the common cold is pathological. We may want to change it because we come to realize that our lives would be happier if we were to have true emotional contact with another. That doesn't mean, however, that the behavior is sick. The way we "turned out" was largely inevitable.

The problem begins in our abject dependence on those who raised us and our deep awareness of this dependence. It is probably true that the closer our nurturing person achieved an optimal balance between support and detachment, the happier the outcome of this drama, but no one escapes unscathed. We are all, to a greater or lesser extent, flawed. It is the human condition. The sooner we realize and accept this reality, the sooner we will get off our own and each others' backs and get on with the business of searching through the rubble of our psychic histories to reclaim our unique capacity to see the world through our own eyes. We will get on the Wisdom path.

Shortly before he died, a few years ago, I had the good fortune to spend some hours with one of the wisest of men, Quentin Crisp.(4) When I saw him he was an eccentric man approaching ninety, an unlikely guru. Just back from England where he played the stage role of Queen Victoria, he sat on a velvet chair, center stage, to be interviewed by one Miss Penny Arcade, an attractive woman in her thirties. The setting was a funky art center on the lower east side of Manhattan. The audience, sixty or so lower east side young folks, mean age early thirties. Prompted by Miss Arcade (an appellation never surrendered by Crisp despite her casually calling him, Quentin), he held forth on his views of life, music, the arts, homosexuality. He was wearing tasteful makeup, a dashing hat and dramatic scarf around his neck. His suit, if I recall correctly, was also velvet.

He was unabashed about his "confused gender" as well as his views about everything. Despite his best efforts, he reported, he was a "dramatic" homosexual at a time when one was not dramatic about such things, and thus, he explained to us, he had no choice but to accept himself. "No one would accept me, and this is what I was; I couldn't change, so I accepted me. It took quite some time but I got around to it."

This was the theme he returned to, gently, again and again: one must accept who one is. Other themes: accept others; treat everyone as nicely as you can, it's just easier that way; have your own opinions about things; challenge but do not fight; yield easily; rest and take it easy; don't be too attached to material things, to mention but a few. All of this was presented gently and with wonderful kindness and humor, no hostility, presence and mild deference. The youngsters were spellbound. One asked him, "Why aren't you a guru, you should be one, would you like that?" Crisp smiled shyly, tilted his head coyly, and replied softly and with a trace of mischief: "That would be nice." The main notion he communicated that day is that happiness is essentially a function of one's relationship with oneself and does not depend on anyone or anything else, and being kind to others is a great help. He communicates this with his whole being. Approaching the completion of his ninth decade on earth, he was totally devoted to doing good for his fellows. Spellbound, I looked at him in his garish outfit, with his unabashedly feminine affectations, and couldn't help thinking what a field day the diagnosticians must have had with him over the years.

Robert Stoller (4) was a rare psychoanalyst in that he studied those with sexual proclivities regarded by society, as well as mental health professionals, as "perverted." His work found them to be, for the most part, just folks who were finding their way, attempting to cope with the vast anxieties of their previous experiences. He writes of his professional isolation due to the enormous prejudice of analysts toward this behavior. Psychoanalysts were just as "perversion-phobic" as the general public except we have been able to manage our own fears about ourselves by labeling behavior pathological, and in this instance, refusing even to deal with it. Another remarkable exception to this aversive tendency is the Paris-based, New Zealand-born Psychoanalyst, Joyce McDougall. In "Plea for a measure of Abnormality" (5) she writes,

> "This book contains a trajectory of reflection on the psycho-analytic experience I have shared with my analysands over a period of many years, for the psychoanalytic adventure, like a love affair, requires two people. It is not an experience in which one person "analyzes" another; it is the analysis of the relationship between two persons. The analyst's participation, forged from his own psychic strengths and weaknesses, enables him to feel and understand something of what his patients are experiencing; at times he identifies with them—the child as well as the adult, and the man as well as the woman in them—while at other moments he finds himself experiencing the thoughts and feelings of those figures of the past who have left an indelible mark on the analysand's psychic world. His most precious guide in this difficult voyage without maps is his intimate if fragmentary acquaintance with his own psychic reality. Thus the analyst shares with his analysand an experience that is in certain ways more private, at times more intense, than his relationships with those near and dear to him." (pp. 1, 2)

McDougall maintains that what looks like normality is often a cover for serious psychic vulnerabilities that only surface under extreme environmental stress. This perhaps explains the phenomena of serious behavioral breaches by prominent men and women in later life. Often the very model of propriety and "normality" an individual, prodded by unexamined shame and fusion and stressed perhaps merely by aging itself, suddenly experiences disintegration of the tenuous, though normal appearing, structure of managing the world. In 1992, a prominent juror, Chief Judge of the Appellate Court of a large state, a man held in high regard by all, a candidate for the U.S. Supreme Court, was arrested and convicted and served a jail sentence for sexually harassing his former lover and her teenage daughter.

Just as "normality" may be a cover for profound conflict, McDougall also points out the opposite: the frequent correlation between creativity and some behaviors that are frowned upon by society including the "perversions." Otto Rank much earlier distinguished between the "normal," the "neurotic," and the "artistic" types. The normal who looks to all the world as just fine is often the most troubled of all. The "neurotic" is clearly vulnerable to the accusation of instability but is actually in process toward the possibility of full human potential, the "Artist" of Rank or the "self-actualized" person of Maslow. McDougall bravely chides us analysts for daring to present a notion of "normal." In her final chapter, which bears the same title as that of her book, she asserts, "Although it is conceivable that an analyst might oppose 'normal and neurotic' it is equally feasible to suggest that it is 'normal to be neurotic.'" She poses the following questions: "Are there any 'normal' analysts? Is there such a thing as 'normal' sexuality? Are there any 'psychoanalytical norms'?" She concludes this chapter and her book with this challenge.

> "Faced with the difficulty of 'becoming a human being' it is always possible to respond by an over-adaptation to the world of external reality, by becoming 'supernormal.' Thereafter the feverish forces of life may become entrapped in a closed-circuit system; these forces, to become creative, must be filtered through the representational symbolic world or their effects may become purely destructive, and when conflict goes unnoticed, even put life itself in danger. What lies beneath this solid protective wall of the 'too-well-adapted-to-life' people? A budding psychosis? Is it possible that when 'normality' is worshipped as an ideal state it serves the function of maintaining a well-compensated psychotic state? There is a growing body of evidence to support the hypotheses that both psychotic and psychosomatic accidents are cloaked for many years in unimpeachable 'normality,' and that the maintenance of this character defense is something of a hazard to health in the event of sudden environmental stress." (p. 485)

Hidden psychological fusion can even be life threatening. I remember when a famous and brilliant artistic creator died at age fifty-three. He developed serious chest congestion and let it go untreated until it was too late. What struck me about this story is that he was surrounded during the three days prior to his last minute rush to the emergency room by his family, his former wife, and several of his children. They said later that he refused their entreaties to go to the hospital. This man, who could probably have purchased the hospital should he have desired, showed up in extremis at the emergency room, without a personal physician. It was too late. The pneumonia had gone too far. He died. A young, brilliant, contributing life was snuffed out. I remember this particularly well because shortly before this another fifty-three-year-old man had a similar experience. He lived alone in a rented studio apartment. At the first signs of the malignant pains in his chest he walked over by himself to an emergency room. He sat there all day and into the night periodically being monitored by the staff until he was diagnosed and treated and sent home. From time to time he called a friend or his daughter to let them know what was going on. A week later he was well. I thought long and hard on this. I wondered who was safest in this world. This latter man had little of what the world could consider security, yet he was able to take care of himself. Could it be that the other man with all his talents and all his worldly goods, and from all reports a fine man, lacked that which he crucially needed at this moment of crisis, namely, psychological separation, though to all the world he appeared psychologically "healthy"?

In "American Pastoral" Philip Roth (6) describes the "Swede:" "I was impressed, as the meal wore on, by how assured he seemed of everything commonplace he said, and how everything he said was suffused by his good nature. I kept waiting for him to lay bare something more than this pointed unobjectionableness, but all that rose to the surface was more surface. What he has instead of a being, I thought is blandness—the guy's radiant with it. He has devised for himself an incognito, and the incognito has become him. Several times during the meal I didn't think I was going to make it, didn't think I'd get to dessert if he was going to keep praising his family and praising his family...until I began to wonder if it wasn't that he was incognito but that he was mad." Speaking of such persons, McDougall concludes:

> "Even though such people rarely turn to psychoanalysis, I would not say that our science can do nothing for the 'supernormal.' The analytic process is itself a creative process, and these individuals carry within themselves all the elements for creating their analyst and their psychoanalytic adventure, like everybody else. If once engaged in this adventure nothing happens to transform their way of experiencing themselves and the world, it may be that we have failed to understand their communication and to detect their cry of distress.
>
> We must also admit in respect to 'normal' people that they are the pillars of society and that without them the social structure would be in imminent peril. The normal man will never overthrow the Monarchy and he will willingly die for the Republic. But analysts, beware! For whom tolls the bell? For them, for me, for you? We may likewise run the risk of dying locked in our identity as "analyst." This is a fate that pursues us all. The analyst who believes himself to be 'normal,' and capable of deciding on 'norms' of behavior for his patients, runs the risk of being extremely detrimental to the creative unfolding and self-discovery they seek. No analyst, according to Freud, may hope to take his patients beyond the point at which he can no longer put himself in question." (pp. 485-486)

Or consider the situation of Martin who had a sore at the base of his tongue. After biopsy he was told it was nothing to worry about. Six months later it had not healed and he returned to his internist who again reassured him, but referred him to a surgeon for consultation. The surgeon recommended it be removed. It turned out to be malignant but nipped in the bud. When I next saw this man he said the following to me: He wanted to thank me for my support, but most of all for pointing out to him in the past that not only would he not be in jeopardy should he leave the self-destructive relationship that he had been in, but that in reality there was a good chance that he would take better care of himself. Martin told me that his surgeon had asked him what had prompted him to come to him when he did. In the surgeon's experience, people generally waited until the cancer had advanced to a much more serious intrusion, and that in those situations the outcome was in doubt. Catching this at such an early stage made the likelihood of such an incursion extremely remote.

The story gets even more interesting. Martin's father had died of tongue cancer. The surgeon said that there was no evidence of a genetic predisposition to this kind of cancer. It was related to smoking and drinking—those who do neither never get this cancer—but not genetics. I pointed out to Martin that there can be a psychological predisposition. We can be so identified with a parent that our bodies can function as if we were actually our parents. I told him that Karl Abraham, the disciple and colleague of Freud who wrote seminal papers about depression, described what happened to him when is own father died. Abraham's hair turned absolutely white as had been his father's. Abraham speculated, and I think quite correctly, that it was his way of keeping his father with him. Martin then told me that his heart attack which had occurred five years earlier was at the exact age that his father had had a heart attack. He also told me that if his tongue cancer was neglected for two years, he would have been the exact age that his father's cancer was diagnosed—at such an advanced stage that he was shortly dead of it!

Psychological fusion can literally be deadly. Reaching out and asking for help means leaving the fusion. It is the breaking of this cycle through psychotherapy and other ways that sets a person free. When one does this the cycle of codependency and fusion in all its manifestations, including bodily ones, can be severed. Contact is begun. A new generation of psychologically separated individuals is born. But it is not because we are pathological and need to be cured by the non-pathological among us. Rather it is because we are fused, filled with shame, and need to free our spirits in relatedness with another who also understands that we are all basically struggling with the same problem. And those who seem the most normal may be the most troubled of all.

So sometimes it is not normal to be so normal, as McDougall reminds us. And it is clearly normal to be not normal. Who is to decide these things and why? We are all trained to feel deficient and remiss or to inflexibly deny any limitations and seek to advertise our perfection. Others of us are compulsed to help others, to cure them of their malaise and are quick to see such malaise, to diagnose it, to learn to understand it, and to cure it. If a person advertises herself as a healer, many will come. If a person advertises herself as sick, many will agree, and promise to cure. Who is sick here? Who is not normal?

Shame

All of us have been abused to some extent, regardless of our upbringing. The nature of human childhood makes some abuse inevitable. We all suffer some shame. Adult life is, then, a recovery from childhood shame. None of us should be ashamed of our shame. We are not alone. And diagnoses can be a shame-fostering thing. There are more than enough people in this world who will be glad to tell you there is something wrong with you. We are all "sick" in this sense, by our very nature. The least sick among us acknowledge it. The most sick deny it. But for all of us the main problem is that we think we are problems. Well, we are faulted, but that's no "problem." Perhaps we can never entirely separate our bodies or even our psychology from the grip of the past, but we can our spirit, for it always was separate and unique, from conception. Our task is to liberate our spirits from the grip of fusion with our earliest caretakers.

Shame is the inevitable situation of humans, and we must accept that. It stems from two sources or is of two natures. The first is the human condition. We are limited in our experience of ourselves, and at the same time we yearn for more, aspire to be more. We all retain some fusion with mother and, thus, have some mother-grandiosity. We think we should know it all and are ashamed we don't.

Second is the reinforcement of shame through human experience. Ridicule about bodily processes or characteristics during childhood is one such source. Attacks upon our body or psyche often create the conviction that there is, truly, something wrong with us. Why else would someone so close to us treat us like this? The dynamics of co-dependency engenders the notion that we are responsible for the feelings or behavior of another, and we must fix these feelings or behaviors or we are awful. We feel shame when we can't and thus tend to control others and the world around us.

Shame is greatly enhanced if, as the child learns that her mother needs to be "fixed," the nature of mother's own defensive system demands she not be fixed, or she cannot acknowledge when she is fixed. The situation gets complicated because in being rebuffed the child learns that it is shameful to "fix" as well. Thus to not fix leads to shame, and to attempt to fix or even to fix is filled with shame. Either way the person loses, and so the shamed person is often depressed. Depression is when two or more choices are seen as the only ones possible in a particular situation and both are unacceptable. Terrorized by such conditions, we feel worthless in our very essence.

But back to the existential feeling of shame. We are, in fact, limited. We make mistakes all the time. We get sick. We are aging. We will die. Is it not important to have compassion? Is it not important to strive for absolute self-acceptance? Is it not important to tell our stories to each other and accept each other and love each other? All of our contacts with our fellow human beings, and indeed even with ourselves, are a mix of compassionate empathy and relatedness accompanied by the distortions and imperatives, sometimes cruel, of our deep beliefs. What we term psychopathology are just the deep beliefs that were our best understanding at the time, and which enabled us to remain in some sort of contact with our essential caretakers.

One of the most poignant of human "spots" is that of a person I knew who had the horrifying awareness that her mother was sadistic and wanted to harm her, even took perverted pleasure in it. This young woman was enraged, "touchy," suspicious, and extremely self-centered. Some might refer to her as narcissistic. She was also lively, kind, searching, and nurturing. Beverly was the victim of profound physical and sexual torture. As the oldest of four children she also felt responsible for her younger siblings. So in addition to the shame that accompanies such abuse, she often suffered guilt feelings as well. She is an extremely moral and righteous person herself, capable of contemptuously condemning those who don't live up to her standards which, of course, included just about the whole human race. At the same time, she was kind to those in need, and particularly compassionate toward the "underdog." Her house was typically filled with wounded animals and people. She was always puzzled and even angry at those victims of abuse who became abusive themselves. It was hard for her to understand how a person might solve the kind of situation she grew up in by identifying with the aggressor rather than the victim.

It was difficult for her to understand another's point of view, in general, because of the fragility of her own opinions and sense of self. She was so battered, and was hanging on to functioning at such expenditure of energy, that she needed to be inflexible to survive. And she was correct about that, certainly at a certain time in her life, and this time felt just like that. It was her psychic reality.

She was most stuck with the notion that her mother meant harm. This was such a disorienting notion to her that she was plagued with desires for revenge. Only "getting even," she believed in her rage, provided the possibility for relief from this anguish. Nothing short of mother's death could free her. At the same time, her spirit had enough room to realize the potential danger to herself of this obsession. When I knew her she had not solved this dilemma. Her paranoia kept her from treatment.

Now, what was so disturbing about the notion of the mother wanting to hurt her child? Clearly such a mother was troubled and was acting out of a solitary pain. Aside from the overwhelming horror of the violation of humanity in the instance of a mother, devoted by nature's design to the protection and nurture of her offspring, actually deliberately harming her young, there was the deep belief by Beverly that such a horror could only happen because she, the victim, was tainted as well. She was tainted by being flesh of this flesh, and she was tainted as the victim. Somehow, this could not have happened to someone who was not herself tainted (profound shame). What Beverly wanted was not really revenge. (She knew this would not accomplish what needed to be accomplished). What she wanted was the mother's acknowledgment of her guilt and her apology! This and only this would remove the taint and make her a valid human being.

Oh, the power of mother! Even such a destructive mother has the power of life and death over the self-concepts of her offspring. And perhaps even more so because of her evil. Beverly, seeing clearly the evil for what it was, nonetheless was in its grip, could keep from being swallowed up by it only by the wall of her paranoid suspicion of the world. She could not separate from her mother even though she had not visited her for years, and she was cursed with the residual terror that a life with such a mother created. This terror rendered her unsure of herself and testy and arrogant, all the while deeply believing she was worthless. It kept her constantly referring to herself to reassure herself of her worth and perhaps of her very existence. More deeply, she was terrified that if she sought psychotherapy, she might discover that she was deserving of her mother's abuse. Then she, not mother, would have to be killed. So she avoided getting help.

Each of us is a survivor. What we are at any moment is our best efforts to make sense of our experience. These are our best decisions about what we had to do. No one can tell us we should have done differently. No one was there with us. No one experienced it but us. If we are sick, we are sick by our very nature, our human nature. In our attempts to survive, we floundered in the task of maintaining radical self-acceptance (more about this in chapter five). What we term psychopathology are all the ways we have gotten stuck in our task of psychologically separating. And no one could have done better than Beverly did. He who says that about another is defending himself against his own self-attacks.

All "psychopathology" is the result of holding on to fixed ideas about life that we developed in relationship to our parents. Mainly it is in the service of not knowing the truth about them. Even blaming them consciously and maintaining symptomatology is really a "not knowing" them in their completeness, and consequently not separating. Blaming one's parents implies they, too, could have been different, or perhaps, it may obscure their actual evil or at least impotence. Giving up blaming means feeling the sadness of the expiration of our childhood dreams and hopes. "Psychopathology" is the strategy to not know (from "psychotics" to "Affect Disorders"), for to know is to separate. To not know what? Who our parents are and what self-betraying decisions we made to stay with the "power" source. To be growing out toward freedom is to be able to tell the truth, at least to ourselves. When we know the truth there is often the impulse to forgive both them and ourselves. Any person who is able to know, and tell the truth, and forgive can never be "sick." What will remain is radical self-acceptance.

In this sense, then, there is no such thing as psychopathology. Each person makes decisions along the way based on his reality at the time. If anything is abnormal it is the traumatic situation which he is bravely attempting to resolve with what his lights provide him. But even this is not abnormal. It is important to know the truth of what happened and to know all one's emotions about that truth. There really is no good guy and no bad guy. It is all the human condition. It is our nature and theirs. We are all innocent. To appreciate this is to be free. But it is hard. No one really wants to live without parents.

Psychology and psychiatry have learned a great deal about intrapsychic functioning, and anyone attempting to help another should learn all there is to know. But even here I must remind us that as science goes, we are babies compared to the "hard" sciences, such as physics. Humans are just not naturally good at understanding how we work psychically and how to modify it. But we do know some things, and it is wise to learn them, ever open to the likely possibility that we will change in our understanding of these things many times, even in our lifetime. A good psychodiagnostician, skilled in the use of diagnostic testing, may ferret out crucial information about underlying psychosis or neurological illness. This happens. Sometimes it is important. Not as often, or as important, as we like to believe and would like others to believe. There is no real test for personal humanity.

In the short history of psychiatry there have been many instances of cruelty by one human to another. In England "mentally defective" persons have been hospitalized, even executed. For reasons of propaganda, the abuses of the Soviet psychiatric establishment became well known to us in the West. Political dissidents were routinely "diagnosed" as "mentally ill" and sentenced to indeterminate sentences in "hospitals." Many psychiatrists were easily malleable tools in such horror. But the United States has not been inured to the isolation of human rights in the name of mental health. In all too recent years people were lobotomized willy-nilly, and in my lifetime groups of persons were considered inferior morally and psychologically. The psychotherapeutic communities stood by and observed. None of us pronounced those who perpetrated such offenses as "disturbed" any more than did the psychotherapists who flourished in the prestigious Goering Institute in Nazi Germany cry out as those diagnosed as inferior to the "master race" withered in the camps of death. (See Cocks, G. "Psychotherapy in the Third Reich: The Goering Institute"). It is a sweet irony that some of those who first arrived at the concentration camps toward the end of World War II were, themselves, victims of racial hatred. These "limited" people, these soldiers who were not allowed to use the same rest rooms as their white buddies, whose purple hearts for valor were marked "colored," those battle scarred men gazed upon those wisps of humanity, those other victims of diagnosed inferiority, and wept.

Who is to say which of us is well and which is sick? I have been around such goings on for thirty years and it does not make me feel secure. We are all very fallible, we humans, and we doctors are no less so for our academic accomplishments. Easily as much evil has been done in the name of diagnosis and diagnostic categories as has good. People and their behaviors continue to defy judgment! And the least of us is often the greatest. The greatest spiritual leaders have come from the most humble origins. Among our present leaders there are so many instances of humble people accomplishing great things. In a more general sense, I see more kindness and gentleness and generosity of spirit and even happiness among those of us more modest in our accomplishments and resources. We humans have a terrible tendency to become less human as we become more "successful." We live in "exclusive" neighborhoods and belong to "exclusive" clubs and organizations. "Exclusive" means to exclude, to think of groups of people as "other than." This human tendency seeps into the mental health arts as well and poses what I consider to be a grave danger.

For it is out of the slimy ooze of the bog that our progenitor, the Snout, came. Who is to say wherein lies the seeds of the next great evolutionary step? Which diagnostic teacher, which pundit would have predicted the Snout? What good could come from Bethlehem? It is the mix of the world that makes us great, and the more we are mixed, the more we are in true contact with all of each other as equals, the more our potential for greatness. Who knows but that our progress will come from the "borderline" personality. It wouldn't surprise me!

I say to the psychodiagnostician and to the psychotherapist and to the "patient": Know each other. Love each other. Respect each other. Help each other. Relate to each other. Understand how each other works. Understand where each is stuck and gently help, if he so wishes, to foster the psychological growing out into the fullness of self, without judgment. Learn all you can of the vast knowledge we are accumulating about various personality organizations. More important, learn all you can about your own. Lead a life of psychological separation and live in your emotions, and then present yourself to another as one who is willing to live with him in his quest. And at the moment of contact with the other, put all your knowledge to the back of your mind and "know" him as the unique person he is, and have an experience with him. This is all the "diagnosis" you need, and without the dangerous possibilities. If later you must translate this experience into the jargon of the uninvolved communication of the mental health profession, be careful not to sacrifice your humanity in the process, nor hers.

Be grateful for the chance. Be humble. And most of all accept yourself fully and appreciate yourself for your brave foray into this most wonderful of human activities.

You know, a kind of trick has been played on us human beings. From the time our parents began to socialize us and teach us the "right way to be" (regardless of how successful or unsuccessful they may have been at it), to our first primers with Dick and Jane and Spot and the perfect parents and mailman and policeman, etc., we have been bombarded with notions of the ideal everything—including the ideals of mental health presented to the public by psychologists and other mental hygiene theorists, quite often these days in 30-second doses. This reinforces our chronic dissatisfaction with ourselves, and prompts our Herculean efforts at presenting an appearance of "normalcy" to others, and even to ourselves. The result has been exhaustion and self-consciousness at best, profound emotional isolation from others and dissociation from ourselves, at worst. How sad.

On the other hand when one strives for a self-acceptance that is profound and radical, recognizing the essential limitations of all human beings, he begins with compassion for himself. He embraces the proposition that in human development, what we term psychopathology is inevitable. What we strive for then is to help persons separate from the standards of others and to reclaim the world as their own. The psychologically separating person deeply appreciates that this is a gradual and lifetime process. There will always be more to do. We will wrestle with our irrational deep beliefs to the very end. It is our nature. Be merciful, and try to have a good time. Stay in contact.

Isaac Bashevis Singer writes poignantly about this: (8)

> "I will muddle through one way or another. I have developed my own theory: not all maladies must be cured. Often the sickness tastes better than the remedy. I am 40 percent deaf, 30 percent blind, 60 percent senile, but I can still read my lectures, repeat my old jokes, discern a beautiful face, listen to the many secrets that women tell me on the morning after my appearance while we drink coffee and munch toast with jam. And when they kiss me before I board the plane back home or to another lecture, I kiss them back and tell them all the same words: 'When you happen to visit New York City, come to see me if I'm still alive.'"

Summary

1. From the beginning of modern dynamic psychology there has been a subtle, but real, judgmental quality to the diagnosis of "psychopathology."

2. Classification of each other isolates us from true contact.

3. Diagnosing denies the positive aspects of a person's behavior, even the "symptoms" themselves, and can further deepen his suffering.

4. What is required is a gentle and humble shared experience of loving kindness.

5. Diagnosis breaks contact. Without emotional contact no therapeutic accomplishment is possible.

6. We must strive to feel in no way superior to our patient. Eschew disdain.

7. What we term psychopathology are strategies of coping with shame as well as blockages in psychological separation. They are the detritus of the struggle between the "demons" of fusion and our innate spirit.

8. How we "turned out" is largely inevitable; we are all flawed; it is the human condition.

9. Many people we label pathological lead extremely successful lives.

10. Conversely, people labeled normal and very accomplished often "break down," perform unpredictable, destructive acts or have unexpected psychosomatic incidents.

11. It is not "normal" or "abnormal" that is important. These categories change with the culture and the diagnostician. It is fusion that often does us in, and the neutralizing of that fusion can only be accomplished by a sensitive and caring non-judgmental exploration between patient and therapist. Our job is to liberate spirits from the grip of fusion with our earliest caretakers.

12. This shame is a universal human characteristic, the deep belief that we are not doing what we should do, even if it is impossible to do it. This leaves us feeling worthless in our essence. Psychotherapy has often made things worse by unwittingly reinforcing shame by haphazard diagnosis and insensitive and confrontational interpretations.

13. What we term psychopathology are just the deep beliefs that were our best understanding as children as to how to remain in some sort of contact with our essential caretakers when they were in conflict with our spirits.

Notes

(1) Bayley, J. Elegy for Iris (New York: St. Martin's Press, 1999)
(2) Eisely, L. Immense Journey (New York: Vintage Books, 1959)

(3) Crisp, Q. Sunday Tea with Quentin Crisp (P.S. 1 Performance Space, 10/18/92)

(4) Stoller, R. Sex and Gender (Science House, 1968)

(5) McDougall, J. Plea for a Measure of Abnormality (New York: International University Press, 1980)

(6) Roth, P. American Pastoral (New York: Houghton Mifflin, 1997)

(7) Cocks, G. Psychotherapy in the Third Reich: The Goering Institute (Oxford University Press, 1980)

(8) Singer, I.B. Interview, Time Magazine, circa 1993

3

Psychotherapy Often Suffers From What It Purports to Cure

My patient, Kayoko told me the other day that she had a strange dream. "I dreamt my heart came out of my chest, and I was holding it in front of me. It looked like the heart that you see on a greeting card, and it was empty in the middle. I was afraid. Suddenly, a light filled the space and shone through it. I looked behind, and I saw that the light was coming from the face of a man with white hair. I felt peaceful."

Scarcely a century old, psychoanalytically informed psychotherapy is one of the most beautiful, loving and unique of all human contacts. One person presents himself to another and invites him or her to say whatever comes into his mind for the better part of an hour. He could say anything, be as critical of the listener as he was inclined to be, in fact he was encouraged to do that, be as honest as possible during this time period. Little of the therapist's personal life and needs would be proffered; rather, the emphasis would be entirely on the other, day in and day out for weeks, even years. Whoever heard of such a thing? When in the history of humankind was this ever done? Even today, when contact with the therapist is scant by comparison with those early years, perhaps a single hour or so per week, what human experience can compare to it? that of spouse, lover, mother, father, child, friend? Who listens like this, so quietly, so long, so reliably?

When I discovered psychoanalytic psychotherapy as a system of ideas, years before I was able to get beyond my fears and experience it directly as a patient, I became a true believer. It was not so much the emphasis on the unconscious and genetic motivation that caught me. Rather it was the notions of transference and resistance. They resonated with my experience of life up until that time, even though they went against the ethos of my down-to-earth, common sense, no-nonsense, Irish Catholicism (1). Yet I recognized the truth in it. Things weren't what they seemed to be. People I observed were operating from agendas other than their expressed ones. People were mysteries, even to themselves.

The idea that we recreated our past in present situations, and that this could be studied in the laboratory of the psychoanalytic consulting room; that the patient would re-experience all the past crucial conflicts with the significant figures of his childhood; that he would resist knowing about this, and that he would fight the analyst/therapist who was trying to help him remember and understand; that, if this resistance was overcome and interpreted, he could reconstruct his past, know the truth and become free, astounded me. This was the greatest discovery humans had ever made! Greater than that of Ptolemy and Darwin, for this was about ourselves and how we function, and why we are so troubled despite our apparent superiority in intellectual functioning. Even today I get a rush as I write this, because in spite of the warts on the body politic of psychotherapy and psychoanalysis that I have been privy to and have contributed to myself, despite all I know about how psychoanalysis really works and how limited we psychoanalysts in reality are, psychoanalysis is still the greatest experiment in human growth instigating contact known to mankind. There was and is hope.

But just as it is normal for plain folks not to be so normal, so too, with psychoanalysts. It is normal for us not to be normal, too, and if there is anything outstandingly not normal about us it is that we seem to have a particularly difficult time acknowledging this.

As I write about psychoanalysis and psychoanalysts I think of Barzini's Foreword to his wonderful book, The Italians (2):

> "I have tried to set down only the most distinguishing features, following…the technique of the honest portrait painter, who puts on canvas those traits which make the sitter the person he is and not another. The sitter happens to be my country, and I have felt at times like the man who does that most exacting of all things, the 'Portrait of the Artist's Mother.' The Mother, in this case, is notoriously distinguished. Her past is glorious, her achievements are dazzling, her traditions noble, her fame awe-inspiring, and her charm irresistible. I have known her and admired her for a long time. I love her dearly.
>
> As I grow older, however (like many sons of famous mothers), I became disenchanted with some of her habits, shocked by some of her secret vices, repelled by her corruption, depravity and shamelessness and hurt when I discovered that she was not, after all, the shining paragon I believed her to be when I was young. Still, I could have no other mother. I could not stop loving her. When I was writing this book I did not want to hurt her feelings, I did not want to be unnecessarily cruel, I did not want to forget her good points; but, at the same time, I tried hard not to flatter her, not to be seduced by her magic charms or misled by my own sentiments. I was determined to do the most honest job of portraiture I possibly could."

This is how I feel about my profession. Like Italy, psychoanalysis is notoriously distinguished, and like Italy for Barzini, psychoanalysis has been my mother. As with the two before her, Helen who birthed me, and the Roman Catholic Church, she has been the embodiment of all my hopes and the love of my life. And as it is with those other loves, I shall never get away, nor do I wish to. They rest in my heart in a place of honor, like ceremonial chiefs of state, to honor and cherish, although they have little voting power these days.

Psychotherapy is a revolutionary, evolutionary advance in the possibilities and availability of human relatedness. With all its spiritual stumbling blocks, its defensive psychologizing and psycho-babble, its corruption into interpersonal and organizational control, it is making possible a new richness in human communication and self-experience. Whether it's most powerful effects are seen in the present or whether its true power is seen in the next generation as was suggested by a colleague (3), psychoanalysis continues to raise our consciousness. It does this socially and culturally, affecting those who never enter a psychoanalyst's office. And it is happening every day all over the world where people are wrestling their demons out in the presence of committed therapists. It is a glorious adventure and, more than that, it makes possible for the first time, as is the case with the 12-step recovery programs, an opportunity to break the chains that have bound us, generation to generation, probably back all the way to that first dysfunctional family, Adam and Eve, some 200,000 years ago or more in fecund Africa. Now there is a chance to break that heretofore inevitable link, that incessant passing on of suffering from generation to generation. Spiritual development, too, now has a real chance, no longer doomed to be strangled in the limiting grip of neurosis and unknown demons, not knowing the devil from the demons.

As a profession we are in a quiescent period. We are still reeling from the lack of the fulfillment of the extravagant claims our hope and our egos prompted us to make. The reports of our demise were premature, though, and probably to some extent reflect the wishes of those who sensed the inevitability of psychological separation as it lurked in our theory. Our profession, itself, does not realize the fullness of the implications of our understanding of fusion and psychological separation. But the seeds are in the unconscious and as we develop and grow as a field, theoretically and in practice, tempered by humility and appreciation of the spiritual, a mighty tree is growing. A recent letter in the New Yorker puts it nicely: "Psychoanalysis, by the way, is not dead; it is coasting. It is watching all the quick-fix therapies fall on their butts. Psychoanalysis is the only method of therapy that is designed to make growth occur in the unconscious, which is the only place growth can take place." (4) (On a more practical note, psychotherapy recently got a big boost from home run champion Mark McGwire: "It took failure for me to understand myself. I'm not afraid to talk about therapy. Guys tell me, 'I'll never go to therapy.' That's bull. Hey, everybody needs therapy. It brought so many things to my life. I can face the music now. I can face the truth.") But there are problems in the profession and practice of psychotherapy and they are serious, perhaps even dangerous.

Malignant Professionalism

Since its origin, the psychotherapeutic experience has been encased in what Masson (5) calls malignant professionalism. The bureaucracy that mushroomed at the beginning of the psychoanalytic movement became so excluding that it rejected Theodore Reik, Freud's "right-hand man," from the first psychoanalytic society because he was a psychologist and not a psychiatrist. They did this despite Freud's clear, sound, and courageous statement on Reik's behalf, "On the Question of Lay Analysis (6), in which he stated that not only is a medical background not essential to being a good psychoanalyst, but rather that the rigidity of medical education might actually be a hindrance. When Reik came to the United States to escape the Nazis, he was denied membership in the American psychoanalytic society. His offense was the same: he was a psychologist, not a psychiatrist. Once more Freud interceded (7)—perhaps he thought his American colleagues would be more egalitarian—and once again he was ignored. "Classical" psychoanalysis is fierce in its exclusiveness (from *excludere*, meaning to exclude). The eminent psychoanalyst and theorist, Anna Freud, Sigmund's daughter maintained that her father would not choose to be a psychoanalyst today if he could see what was going on (perhaps not a "classical" one, anyway!).

I learned of this internecine warfare early in my career. When I was in psychoanalytic training at the Institute for Advanced Psychological Study at Adelphi University, the Institute was defending itself against a suit brought by the Nassau County, New York Medical Society. The crime? Forty years later, the same as that of Theodore Reik. We were psychologists, not physicians. Only psychiatrists should be doing psychoanalysis!

Psychologists, themselves, are guilty of the same snobbishness, however. The Institute where I trained does not admit social workers. Twenty years ago I attended a faculty meeting of their postdoctoral Group Therapy program where I was on faculty. We were discussing declining enrollment, and I suggested we admit Social Workers. The proposal was roundly defeated. I pointed out that we were becoming a Kingdom of Aristocrats, a feudal system with no serfs, and no workers. As such we went down a few years later, resplendent in our raiment, closed for lack of candidates. And social workers are protective of their professional domain as well. Many of them looked down at the candidates of the American Institute of Psychotherapy and Psychoanalysis. This was the training arm of the Community Guidance Service, the largest low-cost psychotherapy service in existence at the time. Its purpose was to provide psychotherapy at modest cost for the poorest and most vulnerable among us. And so it trained ministers and guidance counselors and pre-doctoral level psychologists, each with unusual backgrounds to recommend them, as well as social workers and psychologists and psychiatrists. Carefully selected, many of these persons with non-traditional degrees are among the finest healers I have encountered, and I taught them and learned from them for over fifteen years. But they were outside "the system."

What started out as this dreamy experiment by a brilliant neurologist, following his hunches that something mysterious was transpiring in the "neurological" patients of his day; this great adventure that has captured the imaginations of generations of thinkers and artists, that promised new hope to the suffering and new knowledge to humankind, this challenge to discover the new, to replace the repetitive re-creation of our personal and generational histories with novelty; this assault on the hubris of our psyches, that characteristic of ours that has kept us, as people, morally so far behind our accomplishments, mired in war and racial and ethnic hatred, frozen in stasis despite the transcendent wisdom of the spiritual leaders who rise up from our ashes from time to this—this exciting promise of psychoanalysis—has become overcome by and mired in "the system." Paradoxically, and sadly, our professional structure often encourages the very difficulties that we are dedicated to surmount, specifically, the lack of true contact between people.

Narcissism, again

What psychoanalysis promised was breathtakingly exciting, the prospect of transcending the ego by the very process of separating from the guru (in this instance, the therapist) rather than a lifetime commitment to him! What a leap forward. We now had the spiritual "technology" to analyze and disintegrate those ways of fusion that kept us stuck in self-and-other-destructive behavior despite all our good intentions and prayers. But the disease has overcome us. Our narcissism has swallowed us up. Rather than using our new discoveries to disintegrate our own self-centeredness and become humble, we therapists have all too often taken credit to our selves for the power of nature that analysis of resistance unleashes. Instead of being modest craftsmen who did the work that made possible the self-transcendence of the individual, we became "know-it-alls," clever latency children, fused in our accomplishments with mother rather than working in our own lives to continue the process of separation. Doing our work has even stengthened our personal narcissism, at times, or given us a place to live in it. Our professional organizations can be used by us to the same ends. To the extent this is true, psychotherapy suffers from the very thing it purports to cure.

Narcissism! Destructive, emotionally isolating self-centeredness. As we saw before, this has been our bugaboo from the beginning, both the personal beginning of each of us and the beginning of all of us as a species. As soon as that Snout got to hobble around and expand his horizon from one swamp to another he must have thought he was quite something. Our emerging consciousness, combined with the seemingly endless fusion with the mothering one, plus the unavoidable disturbances in communication right from birth, lead inexorably to this demon, narcissism: the unrealistic inflation of our unique capacities as human beings. And the insistence that we will always be right.

As we saw before, from the beginning of recorded history we have been struggling with self-centeredness. And right from the beginning, spiritual and religious leaders have been telling us to get it under control, and right from the beginning those same leaders have become victims of the very disease they railed against, mired in their own professional malignancy.

Narcissism, the bête noir, of the human race. The limitation that keeps us evaluating ourselves and each other and finding both always coming up short or, in defense, aggrandized. It is the central problem of each of us and leads to the irony of ironies: psychoanalysis, the magnificent philosophy aspiring to free man of his chains, suffers from the same "illness" as that which it relentlessly pursues! And in this illness lies its very limitation. If it is a disease, it is one shared by both doctor and patient, by the diagnostician and the diagnosed.

A certain amount of self-centeredness is good, of course—essential, actually. "Healthy narcissism" we psychotherapists call it. If what is meant by that is self-love and self-acceptance with all one's faults and limitations, then, of course, it is good. It is the goal of life, in my opinion. But that is crucially different from the self-centeredness that seeks to make us seem always right, always outstanding, always expecting adulation and, tragically, unable to love others, appreciate or help them, or to stand in awe of the transcendent universe about us. What's worse is how distanced we are from our own spirits when we are in this narcissistic mode. Self-acceptance or being central-to-self is actually the exact opposite of self-centeredness. It is characterized by a dramatic absence of narcissism of the severe or even more "normal" varieties. It is a consequence of psychological separation, of finding a comfortable and even joyful way of being oneself, free from the enmeshment of one's previous life so as to participate in the Oneness of life that is really timeless. We are simultaneously ourselves in our uniqueness as well as essential and co-equal sharers in all of life.

The narcissistic character asserts that he is magnificent and that he has no limitations and he seeks incessantly for confirmation of this affirmation. The "healthy" narcissist says I am who I am; I am aware of certain limitations but I still aspire to having none. The psychologically separated person, on the other hand, accepts himself exactly as he is and acknowledges that as a human he is essentially limited. While it is nice when others accept him, he rests content in his own realization of this truth, and revels in the shared acknowledgment of limitations by those with whom he associates, and loves. Psychoanalysis has been brilliant in understanding severe narcissism. But toward the other end of the spectrum its own grandiosity actually complicates the problem.

Shame, again

Ernest Kurtz (8) makes the point that much of the suffering of the human condition rises out of our aspirations to accomplish more than we are capable of. He refers here not to personal limitations but to our essential limitedness as a species.

> "To be confronted by one's own essential limitation, to perceive oneself as essentially limited: these are narrowing, choking, tightening experiences. We feel these sensations in our innards, and we struggle against their implications with all our might. But struggle and might aggravate rather than alleviate the pain. Although anyone who has felt that pain can never forget it, the sensation is difficult to name. Philosophers have

called it *angst* or *angoisse*; in English, the dreads of 'anxiety' and
'anguish.' All of these terms derive from the same anxiety
source: ANGH, a primitive root the very sound of which con-
veys the sense of choked tightness gasped when something
squeezes around one's throat. Although difficult to name, this
sense is all too familiar to the alcoholic struggling with his
addiction—the clutching feeling of dread that arises from the
recognition that one is out of control. ANGH is the rub of fini-
tude, reminding of essential limitation.

Alcoholism is an experience of ANGH: it brings home the
realization that to be human is to be essentially limited. The
first response to this reminder is shame. The pain of ANGH
arises, indeed, because something else within "being human"
strives to reach beyond limitation and seeks to impose that one
should not be limited—insists, in short, that any limitation
marks the failure of falling short." (p.11)

Kurtz uses the experience of alcoholism as an example of what he considers to be a universal issue. The realization of our limitedness as human
beings results in the experience of shame. As we saw in the last chapter,
this is true of the "healthy narcissist" as well as of those persons referred to
as the narcissistic and depressive characters and even those suffering with
psychosis. Ironically, it is in the shame of our limitedness that we are all
One. It has been psychology's ignorance of this essentially human form of
shame that has blinded us to the dangers of diagnosis and the importance
of humble searching rather than arrogant and self-protective "knowing."

This shame comes from realizing that you *can't* do; in my view, that
your narcissistic connection with mother has failed; that in some way you
have failed her. This realization is a confirmation of *her* essential limitation
as well. *All forms and traces of narcissism or self-centeredness keep us connected
to mother.* To relinquish shame, to give up narcissism, is to separate—to be
on one's own. One is forced out into the world to look for relationships of
mutuality, not control. One must look outside of self and even "up", to
understand oneself as part of a larger reality.

But none of us is fully there, patient or therapist. It is part of that same limitation that we never reach full acceptance even of our very essential limitations. We are, each of us, struggling along somewhere on that narcissistic line. We say the sick ones have the problem here, but we all do. It is our nature. *It is our excluding ourselves from the narcissistic ranks that proves our residual narcissism.* The truly separated person, relatively free of narcissism, would have no trouble identifying and even chuckling over the manifestations of his residual self-centeredness. It is only our denial of it that is the problem. It is here that we psychotherapists can run into trouble. A friend of mine told me of receiving a call late in the evening from the therapist of his young adult daughter. The therapist wanted to know where his daughter was, since she hadn't shown up for her therapy session earlier in the evening. Alarmed, my friend called around until he located her at a friend's house. His daughter told him that the appointment had been re-scheduled. When he called the therapist back, she said, after a pause, "oh, yes, that's right; I must have had a momentary inefficiency." Most of us would have acknowledged that we had erred. This therapist apparently never erred; she just had momentary inefficiencies.

Denial of our essential limitations, our pride, keeps us psychotherapists suffering and sometimes even getting in the way of the natural growth processes and intentions of our patients. Traditional psychotherapy strives for "cure" and aspires for the independence of the patient. Such aspirations themselves, ironically, deny limitation and thus unwittingly often reinforce shame. The health affirming quality of resistance is overlooked, and slow progress elicits shame in the therapist because he denies his own limitation. The danger then is in "pushing" the patient (sometimes rationalized as "confrontation"). While there may be some cooperative behavioral change as a result (transference cure) there will be little significant and ongoing growth of a significant nature, because at those moments there is no true contact between them.

There are psychotherapists who are profoundly narcissistic, but probably no more of them than in the general population. It is the "ordinary" narcissism that is the problem. Failure to face that in themselves, failure to fully accept ourselves and our humanity, we therapists bring to the therapy the same problem that the patient comes with: self-centeredness. Instead of a compassionate review of the patient's life, informed by excellence of training and knowledge, humbly seeking to release the life potential of the patient, what happens sometimes is a *folie à deux* wherein both participate in a charade with the subtle goal of helping the patient become as "perfect" as the therapist (who in turn is probably trying to become as "perfect" as his therapist or supervisor who in turn is trying to become as perfect as the founder or the leader of whatever psychoanalytic denomination the therapist belongs to). The main activity of healers is to heal themselves. Any presentation of ourselves to the world as healing others and no longer in need of healing ourselves is inauthentic, and to that extent, ineffective. *Healing is the acceptance of self through psychological separation via true contact.* Without that ongoing process in one's own life, the arrival of the patient can be overwhelming.

Joyce McDougall said, "For we do not know what it is that cures after all. We still just have hunches; but my opinion is that it is much more than our intellectual understanding of our patients"(9). Heinrich Racker (10) speaks of the *seidhitze* of the transference, the "burning heat" which must in turn be responded to with a similar intensity by the analyst. When burning heat meets burning heat, such true contact unleashes deep healing. Such enormous power is not readily explained by our theories. Our explanations for these miracles are often "superstitious," *post facto* attempts to make sense of the growth explosion that occurs seemingly "behind our backs." This very transformation, outside our direct control, may be experienced as an assault on our narcissism. Some of us, it seems, would prefer craziness that we could explain to wholeness that occurs without our conscious direction. But "growing-out' is a mysterious process; it defies our need to be "right," our residual self-centeredness; our narcissism; our mother-ego.

The trouble with psychotherapy is that it seeks to replace the control of compulsion with the control of intellectual insight (where there was id, let there ego—in the psychoanalytic sense—be). But *the problem is control itself.* There is much that we can do both for ourselves and for our patients: intend to cease acting out; feel what it is important for us to feel; set the conditions wherein the spirit of the person will naturally do the right thing. But we often stumble for lack of humility. Such humility is the preparation for tolerating, in contact, the ambiguity and mystery of the process until the fruits are apparent.

The Power of True Emotional Contact

There is much that conspires against us therapists in our work. The "establishment," the bureaucracy, constrains us. Our residual narcissism muddies the water. The task itself is an absolutely overwhelming one. Yet many of us persevere, eschew despair, and even relish the task of wrestling with our own demons and those of others. And, miracle of miracles, wonderful things often happen. We sit back and wait. We are careful. We listen respectfully. We study and compare or work with that of others. We share our successes and our failures. We pursue our personal growth. We ask for help. When we don't know the function of a particular problem someone is struggling with, we don't attack it. We know that things will change as they change, and we set the right conditions, open to the possibility that this is not the time for change. We help the patient accept this; again, I emphasize that pushing goals leads to negative self-acceptance and is always anti-growth. The goal is not to get "better" but to fully accept who you are and who everyone else is, and then see what happens. You start telling the truth about your life in the context of *true emotional contact* (11) and the magic begins.

Everyone who consults a professional about a suffering has some sort of difficulty in relating to others. Regardless of the self-diagnosis of the individual, whether it be a symptom, a physical malady, acute sadness, intense fear, uncontrollable ideas accompanied by painful emotions, difficulty in concentrating, failing to live up to an expectation of self or others, the complaints of others about oneself, or whatever, there is always some difficulty in relating to others, some break in true contact, and since the very process of psychotherapy is a relatedness of one to the other, the person's difficulties in living will be present, *in vivo*, from the first contact with the psychotherapist. As will the therapist's, incidentally.

What are the kinds of difficulties a person may have in making contact with another? For two people to have a satisfactory communication with one another, each must desire contact with the other, each must want to attempt to know the other in some way and to be known by him as well.

Probably, if we reflect on our recent communications with others, this level of contact may be relatively rare. But it is wonderful when it does happen. Each experiences a sense of healing and satisfaction. Each enjoys the pleasure that ensues when one grown up makes contact with another. But most of the time, I fear, we tend to go through our day not looking for contact, but rather evaluating each other. We engage each other as parent to child or vice versa. Sometimes this can be pleasurable as when the child, me, gets the approving nod from the parent, you. But even then there exists apprehension for "he who giveth can also taketh away." Grown up contact is characterized by the communicating of ideas and affect and the reception of ideas and affect from an equal. The emotional states accompanying such contact are, typically, excitement, peace, and joy.

Recently, a woman, fifty years of age, consulted me. She breezed into the waiting room with a smile that could light up a room. "How are you," she exclaimed. When I invited her into my consulting room she continued smiling, and made a critical comment about the way the buttons are arranged in the elevators. "How could a short person press the upper floors?" All of this went on before I said a word, and after thirty minutes of my struggling to break through the ways she had learned to "not communicate," to control the world so that people would not discover the horror she felt herself to be, she began to tell me of severe anxiety attacks, shortness of breath and palpitations she has been experiencing since starting a new business venture. She seemed not so much concerned with her health or how to get relief, but rather with how these difficulties affected her image. "I should be rid of all this nonsense at my age." Her life consisted of unceasing evaluations of herself and others. Her solitary business venture terrorized her, and she was critical of herself even for her terror.

How was she to communicate with me? At the end of this first hour I told her that I, too, would be terrified. I urged her to simply observe her feelings and behavior and not judge herself. Her face was contorted with confusion as we parted. But her fixed smile had disappeared. We had begun to make contact. We agreed to meet again.

The goal of psychotherapy is not the achievement of object constancy, arbeiten und lieben, or even an eviscerating orgasm, to mention a few suggested over the years. Rather, the purpose of therapy is to help a person know the truth of her, to help her become awake, to take seriously her task in life, which is to see the world about her and within her and to be happy, to discover ways of going about this that are right for her and uniquely hers. Our work as therapists is not about being smart; it is about being astonished. And to help our patients be astonished.

As time passes a person will feel sadness and loss as little by little he discards old, worn, compulsive, fused ways of being that are no longer necessary. He will be occasionally upset when the dynamics of a social setting elicit his pre-programmed response mode. But he will allow himself to feel, to totally accept himself and others and to live in true contact with them; his disturbing feelings will move through him and out into the ether, leaving him calm again, for the most part undisturbed. He will be able to love and to love persons other than his family members. He will have examined his deepest beliefs, those that may have entrapped him in recreating old familiar patterns of the past in his present relationships. In chapter six I will tell you about Sarah, one of the most exquisitely beautiful souls I have ever known. She once told me, "I learned that it was bad to love anyone outside the family. I shouldn't trust anyone else; no one would care." But, in time, she learned that she really could trust those she, herself, determined to be trustworthy, because her own judgment in the matter was what counted.

Psychotherapy examines the chronic emotions and deepest beliefs we have developed over the years and hold onto fiercely, even though they give us pain and sometimes sickness and death. All of the dynamics of psychotherapy have to do with solving the problem of psychological separation. Resistance is the way we block knowing the feelings and truth of our experience and, as a result, muffling who we really are. Chronic, unexamined affect keeps us living in the past. Transference is the ultimate resistance. Yet, in the cauldron and searing heat of this transference and in the love of the therapist, new possibilities arise.

The new possibilities arise in relationship with the therapist. When both transcend Ego (in the sense of self-centeredness) and relate as fellow human beings within the structure and parameters of the setting, when they truly make contact, what happens for the patient can be a soaring and transcendent experience. The therapist or analyst is no magician, no omnipotent figure. We are more humble technicians, craft-persons, who do our jobs with excellence, relatively free of the patient's opinion of us. We are Ombudspersons of the Spirit. It is not interpretation alone that leads to liberation, not even unconditional positive regard. Rather it is the "sweet spot" of contact between the spirit of the patient as met by the spirit of the therapist. This is relatedness. It is not gratuitous emotionality, but it allows for the deepest and most complete of emotional experience. It is not gratification or indulgence or acting out. It certainly is not a haughty instruction of our patients. Rather, it is kindness, presence, showing up as a searching, growing, imperfect but loving individual. When this happens, the love between patient and therapist, the *seidhitze* that Racker speaks of, the burning heat, is one of the most beautiful loves available to humans. When we make true emotional contact with our clients, we transcend family and personal history, race and ethnicity and gender, our professional pedigree and position in the world, our residual narcissism and self-protective defenses against shame, and healing occurs for each. And when patient and therapist return to family and friends after being together, each is the richer for it.

People frequently ask me, as I am sure they do you, if I am exhausted after a day of "listening to people's problems." Sometimes I am. Rarely, though. And when I am, it is because something of mine has been touched and opened, and I haven't made peace with it yet. I have such spots and they get touched often. Some have yielded little over the years. I am getting better at dealing with them afterward, and so even the suffering can be turned to good purpose. I am forced to face myself daily. But suffering there is. It is not always easy. More typically, though, the end of the day is a happy one. Sometimes I think I am the luckiest man alive. This is what I do with my life, I listen to the struggles of my fellow human beings for truth. The realness, the courage, the integrity, the longing, the suffering, the joy, the love, the triumphs of me and my fellow humans are, in large measure, the stuff of my life. No, I am not weary at the end of the day. When I stop to think of it, I am grateful.

As far back as I can recall, my earliest memories are about trying to hear and be heard. I think I was frightened and still am when the truth is not spoken. Most of us are frightened by the prospect of speaking the truth and having it spoken. Me, too. But more than that I am frightened of the truth not being spoken. I am not sure why. My colleagues would point out my fear for my survival, my fear of abandonment, my lack of trust in my mother. Yes, that is true. But also there is the terrible sadness of not telling one's love and having it told back. I think, despite my neurosis and co-dependency and all that, a place in me, I call it the wisdom place, even as a little child, knew or believed that life without contact was tragic. I loved a lot and was loved a lot, and I wanted to talk about it.

This is what I think I respond to in those who come to therapy. We all want to love and be loved, to nourish and be nourished, and too seldom has anyone taught us how or encouraged our tentative forays into contacting someone else. If I have something to offer my clients it is my understanding of this and having compassion for their struggles. So dear brethren, co-workers, and everyone else, we do this work not just because we are saving our mothers and curing ourselves (and what's wrong with that?) but rather because we are lovers, and if we are not, we are in a dreadful spot.

I had a therapist who loved me and showed it and eventually drove off a cliff in search of a beloved, and I had a therapist who was proper but remote and who was always socially appropriate and a pillar of the therapeutic community but who failed me because he was never fully there. The first left me with unfinished business, but the second drove me crazy, and the result of my encounters with them both taught me that love was the most important ingredient in therapy as in everything else.

Leaving

Psychotherapy ends. I have heard it said that from the moment the first appointment is made between patient and therapist the process of leaving each other has begun. How to leave one another, the problem of life, no? From the moment we enter upon the earth our problem, in a sense, is the termination of loving connections with others and even ourselves. Leaving is a terrible time for everyone, always, all the time. So it is not too surprising that it is often not the therapist's finest hour, either. He must work through his own feelings with his patient.

One day Maurice told me that he was thinking about ending therapy. He felt he was ready and proceeded to tell me all the changes he had experienced during therapy, and now he felt it was time to go. He praised me to the sky. As a paradoxical test, I suggested that if he wanted, we could make the next meeting our last. He agreed. He had a hard time ending the session as he often did. The next session he wanted to sit rather than lie on the couch which he had done for the most recent part of our work, and I said, "It's not over till it's over," and he laughed and moved to the couch. He asked me what I thought of his terminating, and I told him I would give him my opinion but first I suggested he talk about it. He replayed the list of improvements in his life and again asked me what I thought. I told him that his leaving was a personal thing and that I couldn't decide for him, but that I could help him decide, and if he decided to leave I would help him leave. I pointed out to him that separation was a very difficult experience for the therapist, too, and because of that it is often not handled very well, but I would welcome the opportunity to "do it right" with him. He was excited by this and told me that we didn't have to end therapy this session. I said we would stay at it until it was right and until we had exhausted all the therapeutic possibilities in the situation, but that I didn't think it would take very long.

I asked him what was occurring to him. He told me that he was afraid I would disapprove, that what I said was a great relief to him; that he really thought it was time to go, but that it was very hard for him. He was comfortable with me; we had gone through so much together, yet he had some apprehension about his being able to do so well on his own. He wanted to go, but, at the same time, didn't like doing it. I told him that I didn't want him to leave either, but that I wouldn't stop him. He was startled, and asked me why. I told him that I loved him and enjoyed being with him; that it had been a great privilege for me for him to open his heart in my presence, and that I was grateful and would miss him. But I wanted him to grow and supported his leaving 100 percent. This led to a discussion of the role that parents played in the psychological separation of their offspring. Parents resisted it, too, and we examined how this took place in his life. He told me that he was afraid of hurting me by leaving, that he knew this was a crazy thought, and so he resisted telling me it. I told him it wasn't crazy; that it is part of the resistance to separating. Otto Rank called it ethical guilt. Children know they will survive parents, that they know more things about the emerging world, that they will have more and new opportunities. In itself, this reality can be harsh. It is generally complicated by the parents' own separation problems and sometimes even the sabotage of the efforts of their children. Little by little Maurice and I were becoming peers in this existential drama. With a sense of excitement and love and anticipation we agreed to meet again. In a few weeks, Maurice and I said goodbye.

The period after termination can be rocky. In a sense, everything must be re-experienced on one's own to be fully one's own. But if the therapy accomplished what it set out to, when the deepest beliefs, the main idea that has been the organizing principle of one's life has been analyzed and loosened, a calm and efficiency now characterizes one's life. The purpose of psychotherapy is not to change one's basic personality but to gently wake up that part which is asleep, so that you can have all your personality, be all you can be, and enjoy all you can. The way to gently wake the drugged parts is to encourage the person to speak of what he can speak of, and to truly listen; then little by little he will begin to speak of that which he could not speak of. He will wake up, know more of himself, and have at his service the energy used to stay asleep.

Maurice awakened and nervously began life on his own. I felt sad—and joyful.

A person, now unknown to me, will soon enter my office, and smiling broadly to the point of pain, will tell me that the buttons in the elevator are all messed up. "How could a short person reach the top button?" And so it goes.

Summary

1. Psychotherapy is a revolutionary, evolutionary advance in the possibilities and availability of human relatedness.

2. But there are serious problems in the profession of psychotherapy.

3. Our own narcissism and our defenses against the existential shame elicited by our frequent experience of essential limitation can interfere with true emotional contact with our patients.

4. We often take respite in our professional organizations and educational "rank" to assuage these discomforts. This can result in malignant professionalism that interferes with the humble egalitarian contact with patients that is essential to healing.

5. Even just doing our work can actually strengthen narcissism or give it an ego-syntonic place to live. Our professional affiliations can also be used to reinforce this.

6. Many of us persevere and manage to separate psychologically and even relish the task of wrestling with our own demons and those of others.

7. The goal of therapy is to help a person know the truth about herself, to help her become awake, to take seriously her task in life, which is to see the world about her and within her and to be happy; to discover ways of going about this which are right for her and uniquely hers.

8. To accomplish this we must strive for emotional contact with our patients, to become awake ourselves.

9. The therapist or analyst is no magician, no omnipotent figure. We are more humble technicians, craft-persons, who do our job with excellence, relatively free of the patient's opinion of us. It is not interpretation alone that leads to liberation, not even unconditional positive regard. Rather it is the sweet spot of contact between the spirit of the patient as met by the spirit of the therapist. At that moment radical self-acceptance is experienced by both.

10. Finally, helping a person leave therapy without severing emotional contact in the process is, in itself, a powerful healing experience.

Notes

(1) Thomas Cahill in *How the Irish Saved Civilization* claims that Freud said that it was impossible to analyze an Irishman

(2) Barzini, L. *The Italians* (Atheneum, 1964)

(3) Bernstein, A. "Lecture to the Fellows of the American Institute of Psychotherapy and Psychoanalysis" (New York: 1992)

(4) Joyce, J.T. *New Yorker, 9/4/98*

(5) Masson, J. *The Assault on Truth: Freud's Suppression of the Seduction Theory.(Farrar,Strauss and Giroux, 1984)*

(6) Freud, S. "The Question of Lay Analysis" in *Standard Edition* (Hogarth Press, 1957), 20:251-260

(7) _____. "Postscript on the Question of Lay Analysis" in *Standard Edition* (Hogarth Press, 1957), 20:251-260

(8) Kurtz, E. Shame and Guilt: Characteristics of the Dependency Cycle (Hazelden Press 1981)

(9) McDougall, J. *A Plea for a Measure of Abnormality* (New York: International University Press, 1980)

(10) Racker, H. *Transference and Countertransference* (Hogarth Press, 1968)

(11) For a discussion of true emotional contact, see "Intimacy Among Friends and Lovers," in McMahon, J. *Radical Self-Acceptance* (New York: Crossroad Press, 1999, pp.137-164) or see monograph at **www.jamesmcmahonphd.com**

4

What Is It That We Change?

All of life is *recovery from childhood*, particularly the mother-child relationship and what happens to us as *the inevitable consequence of being human* as well as the particular vicissitudes of our unique experience.

Change is return; return to spirit, return to our natures and to Nature, to the Transcendent, to the Other Power, Tariki. It is not becoming something else; it is un-becoming something and becoming ourselves—a return from the false god of mother-fusion to the true divinity of the psychologically separated spirit of each of us.

Paradoxically, change does not occur when we go at a problem head on. Eastern approaches to growth, the "paradoxical intention" theories of the Gestaltists; the insights of Viktor Frankl, all have instructed us as to the paradox that "to change something, one must first not attempt to change anything at all." This approach has not caught on much because it is at odds with our egos, the consequence of the delusions of unexamined mother-fusion. Psychoanalysis has had trouble here because it has relied so heavily on intellectual functioning, "making the unconscious conscious"; "where there was Id, let there Ego be." The main instrument of change in psychoanalysis is the "interpretation" and the main work is the analysis of the resistance to the repressed memories of childhood, the return of which will result in insight and consequent freedom to make new and better choices.

There is great value in psychoanalysis, but it often comes a cropper in that its understanding of psychological change relies too heavily on the egocentrism I have been describing.

My observations have led me to consider three central and crucial factors to be operating in all psychological change:

1. Intention

2. Observation

3. Radical self-acceptance

First and continually, we need to be helped to keep the focus on what we want to change, to examine it, be committed to it. Observation is the study of one's actual behavior as it occurs without any particular attempts to change it. This can be done by vigilance on the part of the individual, by psychoanalysis, by meditation. Most critical is the constant, unrelenting challenge we all, clients and therapists, must make to the self-criticism that constantly barrages us.

Human beings seem always interested in changing ourselves. From the time of conscious awareness someone has been telling us to change, to improve. We go to school to change and learn. Our religious institutions are forever prompting us to do better. We are admonished to forgive others but rarely reminded to forgive ourselves. Rare is the authority that hasn't held up before us the ideal of perfection. By now we ourselves may be willing carriers of that message. We may be urging change and perfection to others. Certainly, in the early moments of the day, when the first light sneaks into our rooms, we are often troubled by some nagging notion of something we have failed to do or be, probably something even deeper. We drag ourselves out of bed gamely to have another shot at it. To make ourselves better today. To change.

As children we naturally aspired to the next step. There is a strong urge toward mastery. It is our spirit prompting us to unfold. Our spirit never stops desiring us to unfold. What a paradox it is that as adults this natural impulse toward unfolding, generally accompanied by so much joy in children, gets perverted into a demanding self-critical abuser. It often comes disguised, this punishing demon, as the helper, the encourager. But it is a fraud. It is not a friend. It seeks not really for joyous self-expression but rather to create and perpetuate a chronic state of regret. Its mission is to keep us in the delusional belief system that to change, to become better will make us happier when its actual motives are to keep us fused with the parental experience of striving to improve in order to achieve parental approval, to be acceptable, to be "good enough."

So we must approach this topic of change very carefully and tenderly. We must begin by questioning the very notion of change. We must start with the dangers involved. We must question why we must change at all. We must look at where within us this change is to occur. Then perhaps we may begin to tease out the factors in ourselves and our lives that may profitably be relinquished. And of course we must maintain loving self-acceptance throughout the whole process or else we are up to something suspect, something other than change.

After all, what is it that we change? It is not who we are. We are who we are, have always been and will always be, though the forms that our selves take are not always known to us or perhaps even understandable. Still, the self develops many characteristics or character traits in its journey of consciousness. Many of these traits are in the service of fusion, and we may decide to yield some as we become stronger and braver and more willing to leave mother to search for the Transcendent in us.

We speak of changing ourselves or changing others or being instrumental in the changing of others. But what is it that is changed that results in different behavior or affective tone? What about the man who is afraid of making friends with women. He would like very much (he thinks) to marry a woman, settle down, and raise children. But he is terrified of meeting women. He breaks out in a sweat every time he speaks with a woman. He generally avoids such situations, but should he find himself there or courageously forces himself into such contact, he is a wreck. He tends to rely excessively on alcohol or drugs to calm him down and supply a feeling of confidence. He gravitates to women who will challenge him less, but whom he finds less interesting and consequently less suitable for him in the long run. What needs to be changed here?

The locus of the problem lies in his deep belief that he is insufficient, not acceptable to a woman he might love and consequently find essential to his existence. Because he cannot satisfy this hypothetical woman (mother?), he believes she surely will abandon him in one way or another. This elicits terror, which is a natural result of another deep belief, that he literally will cease to exist without this woman once she has become so essential to him. The locus, then, is in his beliefs and their attendant terrors, which lie in the self. Compensatory and defensive behaviors are encouraged by the demonic motivation that has as its underlying purpose, the maintenance of fusion with mother. His spirit is neutralized and his self is inundated with self-deprecation, which is encouraged by his demons. Thus his poor feeling about himself goes unchallenged, and the problem is constantly reinforced. What needs to be changed here?

Remember, the unique problem we humans have is that we have developed incorrect deep beliefs and affects which closed us off from the prompting of our spirits. Consequently, the natural, inevitable unfolding of spirit into a unique self was blocked. Our ultimate goal will always be to restore ourselves to our natural functioning, to become who we are, our true selves. Our true selves never need to be changed. Just the opposite; our true selves need to be liberated. We need to "wake up" from the torpor of fusion. Even "orthodox" psychoanalysis understood this right from the beginning. Strachey (1), in a very important article in 1934 states,

> "There is, after all, nothing new in regarding a neurosis as essentially an obstacle or deflecting force in the path of normal development. The final result of psychoanalytic therapy is to enable the neurotic patient's whole mental organization, which is held in check at an infantile stage of development, to continue its progress towards a normal adult state."

So if our friend decides to "change" and he consults a psychotherapist, the first thing that must be done, is to attempt to understand what he wants changed and why. Simultaneously, we must begin to help him restore himself to a condition of self-love; to help him understand that he is stuck, "in the grip" of something; that this is entirely natural and a very human phenomenon. We need to help him to change his faulty belief system in which he sees himself as *being* a problem rather than *having* a problem. This will not be an easy task. We humans do not suffer relief from pain lightly. There may actually be an increase of symptomatology in order to maintain the inner atmosphere of pain. Or the opposite could happen. There may be a "flight into health." He may get "all better." This is a sort of chameleon-like defensive strategy designed to get the observer off track. As soon as the observer stops telling him about the nature of reality as he, the observer, sees it, our patient will revert to old ways. Or he may make impossible standards of behavior so that he will always "fail" and consequently remain ensconced in the familiar inner atmosphere of suffering.

In an atmosphere of unrelenting love and acceptance, the therapist keeps observing and communicating these strategies. Little by little the person's deepest belief system is affected. The notion that he must suffer to be loved, is relentlessly, albeit gently, challenged. Slowly the familiar affects of fear and depression are interrupted by puffs of relief, of peace, occasionally even, by hints of joy. The "problem" is often not so important or has evaporated.

There have been many approaches to change. We have ordered ourselves to change; others have ordered us to change; psychoanalysts have told us that to have insight will free us to change; Gestaltists have told us that to fully experience and express our feelings will lead to change; the cognitive therapists teach us to "think" our way into right living; the bioenergeticists have promised that a direct attack on the bodily manifestations of our conflicts will set us free. Viktor Frankl's notions of "paradoxical intention" suggest that the best way to change is to attempt to change nothing at all; Buddhists, similarly, have advised the loss of self to meditation and the Sensei.

What is it that we change? And how do we do it? Let me share with you what I have noticed. To begin with I will emphasize again the danger in self-attack and abuse the moment we begin to think of changing anything about ourselves. If there is something we want to change or if we are experiencing pain, *we must strive toward compassion toward ourselves as a beginning*. If we are stuck we must infuse ourselves with massive doses of self-love. This is hard because it seems to be our nature to attack ourselves when we are down. Beliefs that we are supposed to be perfect—as defined originally by someone or some standard outside ourselves—are unthinkingly made our own. This, in itself, is often a large part of the problem.

One of the greatest occasions for self-abuse is the belief that we "should" be able to change things by ourselves and that it is some kind of a character fault if we cannot. So on top of where we are stuck we add another layer of pain and fear. All this is based, of course, on an incorrect notion of the nature of humans. We are limited. We are flawed. It is natural for us to make mistakes. It is natural for us to form deep beliefs that at a later point may cause us difficulty. It is our nature!

So it is important to approach the situation with great care and tenderness. It is also important to remember that, whatever happens, *we* will be doing the changing. Whether we go it alone (and a great deal can be accomplished this way, we shall see) or ask the help of a professional caregiver, we are still the ones who will be doing the changing. It is all up to us. We may expose ourselves to individuals or groups or circumstances that maximize our chances for growing out into some behavior, but the locus of change is in our self. Change occurs when we readjust the balance between the influence of the demons and that of our spirit. There is a strong temptation to see the help as coming from someone else and to lose sight of the reality of who really is in charge at all times. Reaching out for help itself is a profoundly independent act. Ironically, we must be cured, in a sense, before we seek the cure. The job will be completed when we realize this.

To change our self involves shame. It involves the shame that prompts us to believe there may be something intrinsically wrong with us because of our "shameful" behavior or because of the abuse we received at the hands of others when we were dependent persons. We had little choice but to react to that abuse with felt shame. But there is also the other kind of shame, that which ensues from the very experience of our limitedness, the kind of ontological or existential shame that abuts our faulted lives. To aspire to change reminds us of this.

For all the reasons we have discussed so far we know there is an enormously strong tendency to remain fused. And despite the complaints we may have about our childhood, there is a realness about that time of our life that never gets fully transcended, an inevitability, as well. We could do precious little about most things regardless of our frustration or determination. We learned that this was the way the world worked and we learned this over a very long time, hundreds of psychological years. Things were the way they were, and there was no changing them (though we could try) and there was no escaping either. Perhaps there was a certain comfort in this inevitability and predictability.

The concepts of freedom, creating our own environment, leaving a self-destructive situation were unknown to us and, in a sense, still are. We have few prototypes for such behavior. This is why change is so difficult for us. On the deepest, perhaps "cellular" level, we do not believe change is possible. It is like discussing psychological separation with a toddler, or computers with an aborigine. At our core, change and psychological separation go against our deepest beliefs and experiences. Yet our spirit challenges us to try. This dilemma I believe has been the theme of the earliest human literature. *How can we transcend our psychological fusion when we have deep beliefs that doing so is impossible?* We have conjured up all sorts of gods and theologies to help us manage this, because we knew deep inside that not transcending it is death itself in life and an unspeakable grief.

To change is to return to our natures and Nature, God, the Tao, Tariki, the other power, the Transcendent, what is. It takes place in a deep, often unconscious part of ourselves, and is not the result of our throwing our egoistic wills at a problem. It is more like surrender, abandoning the ego-fusion motivated patterns of thought and feeling and belief that have kept us isolated from our spirits and what is. It is making peace with the *magnum mysterium.*

If I had to select one word to describe my vocation, I would choose *teacher*. Every aspect of my work—therapy, supervising, writing—is pedagogy of one sort or another. As I became aware over the years that psychotherapy tended to be much too intellectual (the mind being the reflexive agent of our hubris) I paid attention to the ways others taught in other disciplines.

I watched Pablo Casals teach his master class on television on Saturday mornings and I read about Benjamin Harkarvy, the great teacher of the Philadelphia Ballet. More recently I came across F. M. Alexander's technique for postural realignment. Before I read anything about him or by him I took lessons with Betsy Gaw, a gentle teacher who helped to excavate my top-heavy ego-laden head from between my shoulders. and taught me to move it forward and up, delicately. After my session with her I wrote this note:

> Yesterday I had my first Alexander session with Betsy Gaw. She is a kind and related and competent lady who gave me a very good session. As I was laying on the table and she was doing her stuff I kept on thinking about intention and acceptance. She gave me the instruction to let myself be aware of my inner processes at the same time as I listened to her. I thought that this in itself was an acknowledgment of reality because this is the way it is; there is always an inner process paralleling our awareness or responsiveness to that which is around us. I was in an interesting state in which I hovered between sleep, awareness of the relationship between intention and psychological change and responsiveness

to her directions which were, basically, to be aware of body and to "intend" to have body move in the direction it naturally inclines toward, not by forcing it by direct action or will, but merely by intention. It was a marvelous experience and I was excited because it felt like I had bumped into something important for my growth both personally and in my work.

Parenthetically, although I was in a very emotional state that day, at the end of the session I was relieved of any concern save that which was happening at that moment; I was fully absorbed in the present activity, a wonderful activity. As I type this I have the thought that it would be wonderful to have Betsy observe me typing and help me do it right. I have been much more aware of my head and also, even as I type, aware of wanting to do everything "as nature intends."

The Alexander technique is the most gentle and delicate of procedures. As I received the teaching I knew that this was what I was trying to do in psychotherapy. There was such great respect for the person. The person was never admonished to do anything, merely to stop doing certain things. There is great trust in the innate sense of the human organism to right itself; upon study of physical and mental habits, it is gently suggested that the person say "no" to these faulty habits. Faulty habits are not defined arbitrarily by the teacher but rather by what works for the organism and what does not. It is a remarkably healing experience.

In his book, *The Use of the Self,* Alexander (2) explains certain principles of his approach. Using as an illustration a teacher trying to help a person improve his golf game by keeping his eye on the ball when preparing to swing, he reveals the mistakes we make in trying to change.

"To the question why he continues to take his eyes off the ball, in spite of his intention to follow his teacher's instructions and in spite of his "will to do," the answer is that in everything he does he is a confirmed 'end-gainer.' His habit is to work directly for his ends on the "trial and error" plan without giving due consideration to the means whereby those ends should be gained. In the present instance there can be no doubt that the particular end he has in view is to make a good stroke, which means that the moment he begins to play he starts to work for that end directly, without considering what manner of use of his mechanism generally would be the best for the making of a good stroke. The result is that he makes the stroke according to his habitual use, and as this habitual use is misdirected and includes the wrong use of his eyes, he takes his eyes off the ball and makes a bad stroke. It is clear that as long as he is dominated by his habit of end-gaining, he will react to the stimulus to 'make a good stroke' by the same misdirected use of himself, and will continue to take his eyes off the ball." (pp. 50-51)

"End-gaining" is, of course, what we have been speaking of when I urged caution about setting goals and suggested tentativeness in forming intentions to change. On the body level, Alexander discovered what the "paradoxical intentionists" knew and which I always intuitively appreciated, that the best change often occurs when we decide to change nothing at all. Alexander points out that the moment we have an end result in mind a whole set of psycho-physiological expectancies instantaneously are activated. We love these reactions because they seem "right" and "familiar" to us. This is why change of any kind is so difficult.

On the other hand, the use of his mechanisms which would involve his keeping his eyes on the ball during the act of bodily making a stroke would be a use entirely contrary to his habitual use and associated with sensory experiences which, being unfamiliar, would "feel wrong" to him; it may therefore be said that he receives no sensory stimulus in that direction. Any sensory stimulus he receives is in the direction of recreating the familiar sensory experiences which accompany his faulty use, and this carries the day over any so-called "mental" stimulus arising from his "will to do." In other words, the lure of the familiar proves too strong for him and keeps him tied down to the "habitual" use of himself which "feels right."

One night in my therapy group, Buddy was speaking of his fear that a project which he has been working on for fifteen months would be found wanting, that he would not receive a promotion, and that his career would be permanently thwarted. This would be due, in his obsessive view, to the length of time he took preparing this project, some factors he inevitably missed plus the "fact" that he made a mistake in staying in this position when he was offered a lateral move two years ago. The individual who moved into that slot has progressed better than he has, and Buddy is suffering deeply, convinced that he made a stupid move.

Tess, another group member, responded to him. She said that he was playing an old tune, that he kept on worrying about doom and gloom when in fact he was doing very well. He must be getting something out of this worry, she suggested. Granted it was painful, but it had to be familiar. Buddy concurred—and began to berate himself for his not having been able to change this trait despite years of therapy. He pointed out that his father always found something wrong with his performance. If he achieved a grade of 95 percent, his father would demand 100 percent. His father always had his eye on what was lacking. Buddy was correct in his historical understanding. Tess was also right in her observation that this was a familiar theme and a familiar affect. But how to change it? "No matter how I try, I can't seem to make this better," Buddy anguished.

To get back to our analogy with the Alexander method. Buddy's suffering is a good example of the individual's desire to *feel right* in the gaining of his end. Buddy was not really aspiring to end his suffering. He was aspiring to have his report praised, to get a raise, a promotion, and so on. If pressed on the issue of suffering, he would reply that these accomplishments would make him feel better. This, of course, is not the case. None of his many other accomplishments had such a happy outcome.

Buddy is an end-gainer, and as such wanted to accomplish his ends while feeling his old familiar feelings. He needs to be helped to focus on what Alexander calls the "means-whereby," the activities that lead up to an outcome, whatever that outcome might be. Twelve Step programs refer to this as taking the right action and detaching from the outcome.

In operating this way there will be some discomfort, because it is unfamiliar. It is at this point that the battle is joined. The tendency is to employ "will power," an old familiar strategy which is bound to lead us to failure and its attendant regret, the familiar chronic affect of the "bad child." Will power, as Alexander points out, is the use of himself which is misdirected. So what does Buddy do? Tess has made an astute observation. And Greg, another group member, has told him he was wonderful and successful and he should know it. (Buddy loved that, by the way, because it enabled him to get into a symphony of "yes-buts," by which he could drag out his infinite data regarding his deficiencies). Buddy himself was capable of analyzing his behavior until the cows came home and engage in a little parent bashing at the same time, which enabled him to bathe in his old, familiar victim affect. Ah! the good old days.

Just as Alexander instructs his students to say no to the misdirected but familiar physical movements that make it impossible to get the desired end results, I told the group that they must say no to any self-critical statement they make about themselves at any time. They must be vigilant about this. There is no reason that anyone in this room, I suggested, should *ever* abusively criticize themselves for *anything*. Evaluate their behavior objectively? Sure. Regret a behavior, even feel remorse or sadness about something they have done? Perhaps. But never hostile criticism. If they don't like something they have done, they are to have compassion for themselves. When they noticed that the objective evaluation of their behavior was tinged with criticism instead of compassion, they were to say an adamant "NO!" Then they were to say, "I love you," (Buddy, Tess, or Greg)

The group was stunned. You would have thought I had instructed them to do something outrageous, like stripping naked and walking outside. But perhaps that is what I did. I instructed them to strip themselves of their old, familiar ways of dealing with themselves, to say no to these ways and to replace them with a statement of unconditional self-love.

Let's round out our analogy with Alexander. Basic to his theory is the notion that the relationship between the head and the body is the primary controlling factor in improving the performance of a movement, task, or activity. Primary means 1. *most important* and 2. *the first in the sequence of events*. Alexander believes that as he helped a student say no to the faulty ways he held his shoulders and neck that the head would naturally be released. I allow my neck to be free in such a manner that I *delicately* move my head forward and up and allow my *whole* body to follow. From this primary principle, the entire organism, as one unit, would begin to function properly. Automatically, without awareness, our golfer would keep his eyes on the ball, his stroke would improve.

What is the *Primary* factor in psychotherapy, the most important, the first in the sequence of events? *Radical Self-Acceptance*! No one ever changed anything while in the midst of self-hate and self-abuse. This is why there has been so much unsuccessful psychotherapy. On the contrary, we have ignored the suffering of shame by our patients, as psychologist Helen B. Lewis (3) has taught us. As she listened to the psychotherapy tapes for her research she heard *in vivo* the development of rage and shame in the very setting dedicated to the release of suffering. "Successful" cases became unglued and patients returned armed now with psychoanalytic jargon with which to abuse themselves.

The other day a patient of mine complained that she was seeing spots before her eyes and was worried that there was something seriously wrong. This is a woman who has made wonderful changes in her life, but each time she gets rid of one seemingly impossible situation she develops another to replace it. I asked her if she had consulted a physician (I had heard of these spots before, incidentally, in another quiescent moment) and she replied that she had not, that she was afraid to lest she discover she had a brain tumor. After a pause she began once again obsessing about the spots, how if she had a brain tumor it would ruin her life, all would be for naught, and so forth. I replied that she should check it out with a physician and until she did that it was pointless to talk about it. She lapsed into silence and after a few minutes told me that if she couldn't talk about what she wanted to, she might just as well leave; she had no more to say. Upon encouragement from me she told me that what I said is what everyone says to her, and it makes her feel like a real jerk. I was just like everybody else, and if she were to go to the doctor's easily she wouldn't be coming to see me. She wasn't enraged and out of control as she had been in the past. I realized that I had shamed her, and I told her that. We spoke of her shame and what she tends to do with it, and after we had explored that I apologized to her. In my impatience I had lost sight of the importance of helping her say no to her own self-criticism. In this instance I had compounded the problem.

In psychotherapy the primary controlling factor is radical self-acceptance. To try to help a patient rid herself of a behavior that she feels terrible about, without first ridding her of shame and guilt and helping her learn to say no to the knee-jerk, self-abusive but *familiar* ways of dealing with herself is bound to failure and unnecessarily extends treatment. It can even lead to a therapeutic *folie à deux* in which the faulty pattern of behavior is repeated in the therapy endlessly and without analysis. But what I am encouraging takes a long time as well. We are fighting against hundreds of psychological years of faulty beliefs and affects, which are held on to tenaciously because they are *familiar*. To do something differently doesn't feel "right." There is an enormous inertia. We are struggling against an infinity of influences and loves and loyalties and fusions. It is miraculous that we change at all. Certainly, any movement toward the reclamation of the true self must be accompanied at the beginning and always by radical self-acceptance or it is doomed, and we are doomed to remain fused with our caretakers and miss our only opportunity to truly be with ourselves.

Maureen, the woman I just described, had a bout of insomnia several months ago. At the time nothing seemed to help her; she would miss days of sleep at a time. She was growing increasingly desperate. One morning she called early and left a message that I had better do something, perhaps suggest a doctor who could *really* help her. After an initial irritation I realized that she needed me to reassure her that I would be with her and that she was feeling very frightened and lonely during the night. I mentioned this in a supervisory seminar that I led and one of the students commented that perhaps Maureen needed the assurance that I would help her over this difficult time. She suggested I should indicate to Maureen that while I couldn't actually solve the problem for her directly, I would be there for her and would do my best to help her. I wouldn't abandon her no matter what.

I told Maureen this when I saw her. I made some suggestions about how to spend the time should she wake. I told her to write me letter, that I would be thinking about her and trying to come up with better advice, that I would be looking forward to hearing from her in the morning each day, if necessary, until this was resolved. She was reassured and calm. "It's amazing how little sleep a person can get along on," she commented. She then informed me that her mother was a "fanatic" about sleep. Mother was always terrified lest she not get enough rest herself and not be able to function well the next day. Yet when Maureen had difficulty sleeping on occasion as a child, her mother would sit her up on the couch with some warm milk and a stack of books, and she herself would go to sleep. I pointed how abandoned she must have felt, but that now she was a grownup and could survive the hours after her fiancé had gone to sleep until she could call me in the morning.

The following session resulted in no improvement, and I continued the same tack. She spoke of being measured for her wedding dress. I commented that it was sad that her mother, who lived on the West Coast and who was somewhat estranged from her, couldn't be involved. She insisted that her mother wouldn't be interested. I suggested that she might not be quite accurate about that and that perhaps her sleep deprivation was in part a function of her longing for her mother to be with her at this trying time. I suggested that she call her mother and have a conversation with her about having trouble sleeping and also about the wedding, the dress, and all the arrangements. She was skeptical but the next time I saw her she reported that she did call. The conversation was "nice" and, amazingly, the sleep problem had completely disappeared. I'm amazed," she said. "You cured me."

In the midst of her panic about her insomnia Maureen asked if she could increase her hours with me from one to two per week. I had resisted this request previously because she had been doing well once a week and a change in the structure of the therapy is significant and something I do not do lightly. Frequency of contact with a patient, I have found, is an important variable and needs to be watched carefully, particularly in the beginning of treatment. People differ in their capacity to deal with the intensity of relatedness that psychotherapy makes possible. Some need a great deal. Some do better with little, at least initially. The factor here is not merely the fear of intimacy a person may have or his suspiciousness or whatever, but also the extent to which the person is able to tolerate the change in comfort level, what feels "right."

But the analytic work that Maureen and I were doing around the sleep issue and its relationship to her mother's attitude toward sleep as well as her mother's perceived abandonment of her when she was unable to sleep as a child, prompted me to agree to the increase in contact. It was as if Maureen were "allowing" more contact. It went very well. But changes in the frequency are always laden with therapeutic traps, and one day she told me that twice a week was too much for her and she would like to return to once a week. Too quickly I agreed, and we decided to return to one session the following week. When she saw me next, after going back to the old schedule, she was silent. Upon prompting she told me that she was convinced that I hated her and that I didn't want to see her at all and that she was a royal pain in the neck to me. She interpreted my acquiescence in the reduction of hours as a rejection and an abandonment. I agreed with her that I was insensitive and told her that I really did want to see her twice a week. She was visibly relieved and the next two weeks were very productive. This was the period in which she contacted her mother and experienced the instantaneous and complete removal of the symptom. Two weeks later she again asked to reduce the frequency of contact. "I don't feel comfortable coming this often." Learning from my previous mistake, I told her that I thought we were doing well at this rate and that I would like to explore with her what was going on inside that prompted her to want to reduce the number of times we met. Just what was it that she was uncomfortable about?

She said that she didn't know, but that we had been doing fine before, that she liked the pace, that this was no longer an emergency. I told her I found it interesting that she would allow herself more contact with me in an "emergency" but not merely to make her life better and possibly get the job done quicker. She was "comfortable" in getting the help she needed if she was in crisis but not comfortable in getting help to thrive! We then had an excellent session in which she reported material to me that she never had in the past. "Is it necessary to 'dwell' on all these painful memories?" she asked. I replied that it was, if she were to truly get well and be happy. Besides, she was "dwelling" on them all the time anyway, but when it was chronic pain and not acute suffering she not only could tolerate it but was actually more comfortable. The two things she couldn't abide were excruciating pain *or* feeling better!

In the course of that session Maureen described to me some of the most painful experiences I have ever heard. Her life had been riddled with suffering. This is what she knew. This is what she was comfortable with; this is what felt right to her. As she began to return to her self, it didn't feel right to her. She was prepared for an accommodation, but not to fly. And this is why change is so hard. Maureen, at least, had put herself in a situation in which she, with my help, could observe herself and her life, the consequence of all the decisions she had made in her life in order to save it. Shouldn't one celebrate oneself for that?

What we have going against us is so enormous that it is tempting to wonder whether change is possible at all. When we consider the world about us and how little we, as a species, have changed from biblical times, for example, it makes one wonder. Today we are fighting wars just as we did at all times that we know about. It is our nature, many cry. That is the way it is. Are we "fixed" by genetics and perhaps early infant experiences, perhaps even in the womb? Can we go from "deficient" to "normal"? Can we go from "normal" to "better"? Can we go from "better" to "transcendent"? Can the average person become "enlightened"? Are we "destined" due to biology and previous psychological events? Are all the psychoanalysts and spiritualists deluded? Are all these aspirations mere illusions, just balm to salve another narcissistic wound? Sometimes it sure looks that way.

Along these lines is the age-old question of whether humankind is essentially good or evil. Right from the beginning we seem to have assumed that human beings are intrinsically evil. In the Christian tradition, we must have a savior in order to be or do good. I think the question itself is an indication of the "spot" we poor humans are in. The concepts of good and evil could only be created by man because of the uniqueness of our consciousness. The categories of good and evil are man-made ones; evaluations started with man (although we often project them onto God). Animals and all other living things have no such concepts; they just do what they do, what is natural for them to do. When we ask the question are we good or evil, this is, in a sense, a trick question. The categories in themselves are artificial, not natural. We created them to exercise our capacity for evaluation.

A better way of posing the question, it seems to me, is to ask to what extent what we do is *natural*, or necessary to maintain survival. This is complicated for us because of consciousness and because of the *awareness* of danger and consequent fear. This fear leads to all sorts of behavior, some of which may be labeled evil. The fear itself is not unnatural, but our consciousness leads us to strategies, many of them incorrect or distorted, and consequently to behavior unnecessarily destructive to others or self. So evil is a possibility; but it is not our nature. Similarly, with love. The same consciousness and capacity for evaluation and judgment lead to identification with and empathy for others. There has evolved what appears to be a distinctly human characteristic, love. We can love, and we can be afraid and finally we can choose. Man, then, is neither good nor evil. We are persons with consciousness, and consequently the capacity for fear, error, love, and choice.

One of the reasons change does not seem possible is because of our experience with how hard it is to accomplish. Change is so very hard for two reasons. The first is the depth of fusion. The second is that we humans have been going about change in the wrong way. When we are in the "grip" of something, there are several layers of psychic events involved. The first layer includes those things we are immediately conscious of. "Below" that are those things that are not immediately conscious but can readily be summoned into consciousness. Third, there are those things that are deeply imbedded in our "unconscious" and which are hard to access either because they got there so long ago that they may not be expressible in verbal language or because there are active mechanisms in our mind that serve to keep these "dangerous" ideas and emotions out of awareness. It is in these three layers that we typically work to effect change.

What is not generally realized, both within and outside of our profession, is that there are many other strata, or "lines of music" as I like to think of it, that are even deeper than what I just described. Even further below is the life and death struggle that goes on between spirit, trying to get breath and move forward, and the demons that have the self in its "grip." This battle is deep and continuous. *This struggle involves all the systems of the organism: biological, muscular, emotional, hormonal, vegetative— many non-verbal. The conscious, intellectual, ethical, moral activities of the higher level are often no match for it.* Sometimes the best we can do is simply experience the struggle—do nothing, roll with the punches, sometimes give in. But spirit will always prevail if we persevere.

In chapter six you will meet Sarah. Her body was compromised throughout her struggle to return to herself. She was struggling with candida during her treatment. She also told me that she had stopped growing at the onset of puberty. As the therapy progressed she reported that growth returned. Her hips were broadening; her breasts started to grow.

> I'm walking differently, I can sing, my eyes are improving, my nose is clearing. The muscles in my face were all rigid and now they are relaxing. My feet were deformed and now they are improving...as each symptom disappears, I'm remembering when it first started.

I once asked her if she believed the candida was a result of depression or if the depression was the result of her chronic physical problems.

> I've been thinking about that a lot...I think that very early it was important psychologically. When I was very small I somehow sensed that being totally healthy in my family was just not going to work...that sounds terrible, I know...*but I could not have grown up healthy in my home*...it's like sleeping beauty...it's connected to the depression...the constant interaction. This stuff began to break down after my mother died...I'm having a delayed puberty...the whole way we lived is a function of depression.

How do we fight such influences? Psychoanalysis suggests "insight"; non-directive therapists suggest unconditional positive regard. All forget we are working against hundreds of psychological years of conditioning and the creation of deeply embedded "deep" beliefs. Will one, two, or three hours a week of psychotherapy modify these influences and loose the spirit?

Change has been difficult for us, particularly in Western cultures, because of the failure to appreciate the depth and complexity of the human psyche and spirit. The classical Freudian model of the structure of personality, Id, Ego, and Superego, as far reaching as it is, still envisions an inner life much more shallow than it truly is. This was because of the scientific *Zeitgeist* and the love affair we were having with the human mind and its presumed capabilities. In its "cultural revolution," psychoanalysis willy nilly cast off the life and death struggle between spirit and demons in an attempt to make the complexity of the psyche, as it was emerging through the brilliant technology of free association, manageable for examination and study. We *had* to understand; we *had* to control; we *had* to have a conscious, self-directed technique of eliciting change.

But that is not how we work. We work the way the animals work, the way the trees work, the way all living matter works. We make the understandable mistake of assuming we worked differently because our minds are capable of doing some things much better than the animals and the trees. But this is a big mistake. The human mind is as much a trap and a snare as it is a worker of miracles. It is getting this total awareness of mind in focus that is our task.

It is our very mind, our consciousness and two other crucial factors, our long childhoods, and flawed caretakers, that have resulted in the deep primordial unconscious struggle that each of us is engaged in, that is, between the demons of fusion and the push toward the transcendent by the spirit. This is where the salient struggle goes on, not on the upper strata of the more superficial characteristics of the person, such as consciousness and conceptualization. The crucial thing is not merely to understand, to master, to consciously effect change, but rather to find ways to help our total person get aligned with that which transcends, not our humanness, but our narcissism. Intellectual understanding and some of the other techniques or procedures may indeed be helpful, but without an appreciation of where the battle is actually joined and what the proper goal of psychotherapeutic mediation should be, it is as much a danger as a panacea, as much a troublemaker as a healer.

Yes, there is enormous resistance to change. When people approach separating from their chronic selves, whether patient or therapist, when they consider surrendering that which they know and are *familiar* with, there is panic and the tendency to trip oneself up so as to return to the known. I refer to this as the "call back." As soon as we change we experience a call back into our old ways. This is a crucial moment and one which requires vigilance. Just as a person running a marathon often comes up against a wall of resistance at about the twentieth mile, so too, in an ongoing serious encounter between therapist and patient there is often a final barrier that seems impossible to surmount. The wall can take the form of physical illness, accident, severe acting out, or frequently, a premature ending of therapy. Sometimes people have to "fall apart" before they can put themselves back together in a better way for themselves. (I prefer to think of this as a breakthrough rather than a breakdown.) Yet the movement into the new is not entirely unknown. There have been happy glimpses of it throughout life; otherwise it probably would be impossible even to aspire to. But the lure of the chronic self is always lurking about.

The therapist, too, has to hold a steady course at this point. In fact, any time a therapist is making a deep, meaningful observation (a mutative interpretation as Strachey calls it) (4), he must open himself to his inner demons.

> "All of this strongly suggests that the giving of a mutative interpretation is a crucial act for the analyst as well as for the patient, and that he is exposing himself to some great danger in doing so. And this in turn will become intelligible when we reflect that at the moment of interpretation the analyst is in fact deliberately evoking a quantity of the patient's id-energy while it is alive and actual and unambiguous and aimed directly at

himself. Such a moment must above all others put to the test his relations with his own unconscious impulses."

Both therapist and patient have the same problem. Each is assuming that he truly lives in those three strata of mental functioning that I described above. But each is really comprised of more layers of psychic functioning; each is using or not using these many other strata to gain or detriment, with some awareness of this or not. It is similar to the nature of reality itself. We assume that reality is comprised of those layers that we happen to notice. Some of us seem to notice more of reality than others do. But the most aware of us are still noticing only a small part of what reality is. Reality is infinite. There are infinite layers of reality.

We operate only within the first few layers. We consider those events that we don't understand to be "miracles." They are actually events of a further realm of reality that we serendipitously bump into. Since our personality is just another instance of infinite reality, our flawed and limited consciousness renders us incapable of understanding much of what happens within us. This is disappointing to those who feel they must know everything or those who must control everything. The good news is that when we get out of our own way, everything works just fine as does the universe. The difficulties in our functioning are largely man made. Our difficulties in changing are man made, as well. Change is nothing more than our *stopping* doing those things which keep us from functioning on nature's agenda. When that is done, we get back on track and great things happen. We permit the winds of Tariki to push us along, as Itsuki (5) teaches us.

After a period of experiencing and expressing the despair that underlined her compulsive cheerfulness, the woman I described in the previous chapter who criticized the layout of the floor buttons in the elevator, began to experience promptings from deep within her. She told me, "There is a woman inside myself that I didn't know was there…she is standing up for herself…she is speaking to people in a way I didn't know was possible." She was excited. Other times she is frightened because this Person inside her that is surfacing is threatening to the deep belief system that she has lived with all of her life. She is realizing that she can take care of herself and live life on the promptings of her spirit. She no longer needs to pay keen attention to what others want of her so that she will be loved and will not die. Nor does she have to be secretly enraged at such an arrangement.

When change occurs in psychotherapy it is because patient and therapist have touched each other in a place that emanates from deep within each one. Both must change and both must have the courage to let this change happen without fully understanding how it comes about. Change *is* possible. Growing out into our selves is an exciting adventure. But it does not involve force or mechanical shuffling things about. It mostly involves surrender, a yielding of narcissism and mother-fusion to make room for the life-affirming spirit to arise from the ashes within. Will power has nothing to do with it, save our physically getting ourselves to the places where our spirit has a chance. Will power is directed at behavior, and there is always a much stronger internal and unconscious imperative working against that. Besides, will power is always in the service of ego (in the colloquial sense) and ego, alluring as it is, cannot bring us to our selves. Even in an instance where will power results in change of a behavior, I suspect there is actually something else going on at a much deeper level. Spirit is being tapped, or else the change is accomplished at an enormous price in repression and truncation of spirit.

Change, actually, should be easy, joyous, and gentle, accompanied by sweetness and peace. Change begins with the intention to accept ourselves fully, to realize the enormity of the resistance to our becoming fully our selves. It involves, in addition, a humble beginning of reliance on a power outside ourselves, the *magnum mysterium,* which gently births our awakening self. As far as I can determine, there are no one-to-one interventions that lead directly to change, though sometimes a particular interpretation or intervention may help a person ease over the line into a new way of being. More typically, there are parameters of behavior that set the context in which a person has a better chance of getting on the Wisdom path. In the following chapter I will explore three general characteristics that seem to me to help change along.

Summary

1. Change is not becoming something else; it is unbecoming something and becoming one's true self.

2. Change does not occur by attacking problems head on.

3. Three crucial factors operating in all psychological change are: intention, observation, and radical self-acceptance

4. Our true selves need never be changed. Just the opposite. Our true selves need to be liberated. We need to "wake up" from the torpor of fusion.

4. It is crucial to work with the person's self-attacks and abuse. Such undoing accelerates the moment we begin to consider changing anything about ourselves.

5. The Alexander Technique of Postural Realignment is discussed as an analogy to the process of psychotherapeutic "realignment."

6. The primary factor in change in psychotherapy is radical self-acceptance. Some therapists have been ignorant of this and have unwittingly ignored the suffering of shame. In some instances, we have actually exacerbated it.

7. Change, in itself, feels unfamiliar. It can be disorienting and our patient needs support with this discomfort.

8. Humans are neither good nor evil. We are persons with consciousness, and consequently we have the capacity for fear, terror, love, and choice.

9. Change is so hard because the struggle between spirit, trying to breath and move forward, and the demons of fusion that have the self in its grip, is so deep and continuous.

10. This struggle involves all the systems of the organism: biological, muscular, emotional, hormonal, vegetative—many non-verbal. The conscious, intellectual, ethical, moral activities of the "higher" levels of psychic activity are often no match for it.

11. Sometimes the best we can do is simply experience the struggle, do nothing, roll with the punches, sometimes give in. But spirit will always prevail if we persevere in intention, observation, and radical self-acceptance.

12. Change occurs in psychotherapy because patient and therapist have touched each other in a place that emanates from deep within each one. They have experienced true emotional contact. Both must change and both must have the courage to let this change happen without full understanding of how it comes about, by surrendering, humbly in a sense, to the unfathomable mystery of the transcendent universe.

Notes

(1) Strachey, J. "The Nature of the Therapeutic Action of Psychoanalysis," in *The Evolution of Psychoanalytic Technique*. eds. M. Bergmann and F. Hartman. (Basic Books, 1976)
(2) Alexander, F.M. *The Use of the Self.* Long Beach, Calif.: Centerline Press, 1985; originally published New York: E.P.Dutton, 1932.
(3) Helen Block Lewis, in Karen, R. "Shame." *Atlantic Monthly* (February 1992), 40-70

(4) Strachey, J., *ibid.*
(5) Itsuki, Hiroyuki. *Tariki.* (Tokyo: Kodanshka Ltd: 2001) p.xvii

5

How Change Really Occurs

A Therapist's prayer:

May I accept myself today just as I am. May I accept my changing today, just as it is. May I be present to my patient today just as he is; may I accept his changing just as it is.

We know that nobody really wants to change despite our constant haranguing of ourselves and each other. Nobody *can* change either, at least in the way we are told we should. Isn't it a joyous reality that we don't have to?

What we call change is return. Return to the natural growing out of self with which we entered life, and which always operates no matter how stuck we may be at the moment. The spirit keeps moving us along, although sometimes there are weighty obstacles. Releasing the spirit is what we're after, finding a way to return to our true selves, permitting the growing out into ourselves to happen in a fuller and more free way.

In this chapter we will discuss the three ingredients I believe to be essential to all growing out. If you look close enough you will find these ingredients in all *successful* methods that people have employed to help each other. I know that as you become more deeply aware of them you will grow out more into yourself, and you will help those who consult you to do likewise. The deep understanding and appreciation of these ingredients will help you in what I hope now is a conscious intention of yours: to release yourself from the grip of your earliest caretakers and to see the world with your own eyes.

Intention

It seems logical that if we want to change something we should know what it is that we want to change, and have the intention to change it. But it is not always so simple. We may not really want to change but rather may be yielding to the wishes of someone else. Or perhaps it is not someone else in the present, but the wishes of someone from our past, someone that we have made part of us. We may have accepted standards of behavior that are actually at odds with our spirit. So on the conscious, expressed level or deeper, there may be conflict in even our intention to change.

I think most of us deeply accept ourselves in the sense that we know ourselves and understand, at some level, that we are what we are largely because we chose to be or felt we had to be. But we generally *don't* accept ourselves in the sense that we accept that acceptance of ourselves. We deeply believe that we must be the way we are, yet we judge, condemn, and generally make ourselves miserable. That whole process may, in itself, be part of what we believe we are and must be. We may feel we have to be miserable, and we can use the discrepancy between what we feel ourselves to be and what we believe we should be to torture ourselves.

So when we want to change something we have a dilemma. We often go to the "helper" to define what needs to be changed, while at the same time we have a deep belief that no change is possible, or we get into a delusion that this helper is going to magically accomplish something. The therapy situation, then, is fraught with impossibilities from the outset. It has implicit in it the seeds of failure and increased feelings of worthlessness. Why should we ask ourselves to change, particularly if we believe, perhaps in some deep recess of our souls, that what we are at any particular moment in time is our best judgment of how to be?

The immediate problem that must be dealt with by the helper, it seems to me, is why the person believes he must change and the profound lack of self-acceptance that this implies. If the person indeed wants to change something about his behavior, then why does this discrepancy between the expressed intention of the person and his actual accomplished behavior exist? Flavoring this inquiry will be the pervasive self-condemnation that most of us carry with us at all times. With a little luck and massive good will there may arise a relationship of true contact between the two parties that will enable the study of the individual in a loving and accepting context. This may result in *his* juggling around some of the variables inside of himself which have prompted his behavior. All this may result in new decisions and new behavior we call change. This may come from a place so deep in the person that the activating variable may never be consciously known to either party, and both must accept this with humility.

The helper, for his part, must have as his intention not placing his values on the person consulting him. This is where Carl Rogers was so brilliant. He focused *entirely* on the inner experience of the client. Even interpretation was avoided. Although interpretation was the chief agent of change for Freud, he, too, in his "abstinence" was careful not to impose his opinions on the patient. Even the interpretation, if done correctly, should just bring the patient that little bit of awareness that he himself had gotten to by dint of painstaking examination and analysis of resistance.

One of the difficulties in goal setting is the implication that the achieving of the goal will provide happiness. Even when the goal is achieved, happiness is not necessarily the by-product. Sometimes just the opposite occurs. I knew a man who ardently believed that once he became a millionaire all his problems would be over and he would be happy. When he achieved his goal, he did not become happy; he worried even more about the preservation of his newfound wealth and then became more depressed because he discovered that what he had worked so hard for all his life did not make him happy.

Happiness is a function of a person's relationship with himself as Quentin Crisp was fond of saying. When Christ said it was harder for a rich man to be saved than for a camel to get through the eye of a needle, perhaps he was referring to how few millionaires seem happy. In fact, when happiness is seen as depending on *anything* outside one's relationship to one's self (and his Transcendent, "inside him and around him"), the project is doomed to failure. This is also true for psychotherapy. We need to make sure *why* a person wants to change and examine first the implicit self-condemnation in these aspirations; make clear that the change in itself may not result in happiness; be ever mindful of the changing nature of intentions and the ever-present danger of their use in the service of demonic self-hatred, for if there is anything that will absolutely prevent growth and expansion of the self, it is self-condemnation. This is the beginning of your client's development of radical self-acceptance.

I was discussing this with a 36-year-old art director one day. I was pointing out to him that our behavior at any moment is the end product of the best information and meaning we have available to us at any particular time. If this is at odds with our conscious intention, it is because we are just not fully aware of that part of us that is influencing the decisions. Rather than criticize, it is time for loving observation. Criticism comes from the demons, which do not want us to grow out into the fullness of our being.

> Walter: I just realized that the critical voice is my father's.
> Me: Can you live without your father on your back?
> Walter: I don't know.
> Me: It means separating from your father.
> Walter: I always believed that if I silenced it, its power would show itself in other ways…I'd fuck up without a word, in even worse ways.
> Me: If left to your own devices.

Walter: I don't know…I never even considered living my own
life.
Me: That's what seems to be at stake here.

The trouble with bio-energetics, rational emotive therapy, and certain
self-help approaches like neuro-linguistic programming and inspirational
offshoots is that they assume that to "know" something about how the
mind and human behavior work enables us to "do" something based on
that knowledge, to "improve" ourselves or "accomplish" something or
"control" our feelings. Control is the key concept here. So we throw ourselves at our problems, and we often fail because we have not dealt with
intention. And when we fail, our self-esteem actually gets worse. Even
when we think we know what we are aiming at we may be mistaken. If a
conscious, logical, rational goal is not accomplished, it may be for many
reasons, some of them better for the individual than the conscious
"owned" one.

Nature has its own plan for us. Sometimes a psychological conflict or
inhibition may be a protection against a physical, life-threatening illness
that the individual is not aware of. Alcoholism, for example, is, on some
rare occasions, a defense against a more malignant psychotic process that
blooms when the alcohol is withdrawn. Schizophrenics have been shown
to have a lesser incidence of malignant cancer than the general population.
These are extreme cases, but I mention them to remind us that we must
have humility in developing goals. If we do not have this perspective, the
process of attempting to change may unwittingly become the very agency
of torture that the attempt to change was designed to correct.

Let us return to our man in the previous chapter, who was fearful of
women. By forming an intention to understand his relationship to women
with no specific goals in mind other than that, and by observing his behavior and, of course, by radical self-acceptance, he noticed he was attracted to
ungiving women. He would become involved with such a woman and even

when he realized he wasn't getting much nurturance, he found himself unable to separate from her. He then began a typical repetitive pattern of attempted resolution. First, he tried to change her by relinquishing his own needs and being so "good" that he believed that she would have to be nice to him. When that failed to get the desired results (as it inevitably did), he changed strategies. He rapidly ran through the sequence of becoming more demanding, then angry, and finally depressed. Or he would explode and the woman in question would get rid of him. Over time we discovered his penchant for self-centered and narcissistic women and his *compulsion* to remain in an unsatisfying relationship. In compulsively replicating his relationship with his mother, *an ungiving, narcissistic woman, whom he indeed could not leave*, he maintained his internal, familiar psychic experience. As he more deeply experienced the "grip" he was in and shed the nagging self-criticism that generally accompanied this realization, it began to weaken its hold on him. He began to experience deeply his new understanding of what was going on inside him. He gradually and gently let go of the deep beliefs and chronic affects and was able, for the first time in his life, to be available to a more giving woman. He was separating psychologically.

If our intention is to understand who we are in our relatedness to the world, each bit of discovery can be received with a tender and delicate respect. We need not be too quick to improve. Improvement, after all, is only a hypothesis. You do not know what purpose a symptom may serve. We must be humble. Then we may step up to pain, shame, our deepest beliefs, and learn to dance with them. Fully experiencing the trap we are in begins the process of dissolution. The invocation to change is, in a sense, an aggressive thing; growing out into oneself is better considered as a gentle matter, suffused with love and acceptance and softness, like the birthing of a baby, messy but joyful.

In therapy you may notice the changing nature of intention. What we came to treatment for is rarely what we wind up understanding as the most significant issue. After a while, the charge to change, the demand to change, even the wish to change evaporates. We become totally absorbed in being, and knowing who we are, and loving that.

Observation

At the end of an initial interview with new patients I suggest this. I urge them to put aside their desire to change for the time being and focus rather on observing themselves and their life. In the time until the next appointment I encourage them to become "watchpersons" of their lives; to merely "notice" what they do and how they feel; how it is between them and others; what actually happens. I tell them to try not to judge themselves but to observe that too, if that is what they do. Inevitably the next session is miraculous. For most, it is the first time they have paid attention to who they are and what they do, at least for a very long time. Each begins the journey of fascination with one's own processes. Most of us have never been encouraged to do this and, perhaps, have actually been discouraged from it. Try it yourself. Spend a week just noticing yourself and what you do and what you feel and how it goes between you and others. It will be a fascinating experience.

Stephen Levine (1) wrote:

> "It is in letting go of old models, opening into 'don't know,' that we discover life. It means getting out of our own way in the same manner that a healer gets out of his own way and lets the extraordinary nature of the universe manifest through him. He is not doing anything. As a matter of fact, for a moment his self-oriented doing has ceased so that he may become a conduit for the energy of wholeness. So, too, in the openness of "don't know" we watch the healing come about. We experience the melting away of old knowings and expectations. We begin to experience the joy of simply being, in love with all that is.
>
> When we no longer cling to our knowing, but simply open to the truth of each moment as it is, life goes beyond heaven and hell, beyond the mind's constant angling for satisfaction."

It is another one of our limitations as humans that there is interference in this natural, essential tendency to notice and explore our worlds. Observe the infant. She is totally absorbed with the world, in looking, making judgments, delighting in her new discoveries. In our misguided love and ambition for her we often interfere. We tell her the names of things, we tell him what to look at and what not to, we solve the problem for him when a little patience would enable him to do it himself. And we teach him evaluation from the beginning. This is "good" and this is "bad." Thus the process of exploring the world is immediately contaminated.

Most animals explore while their mothers protect. Being human often interferes with the natural exploring tendencies that facilitate trust in independent perception. As a result, most of us remain in a child relationship to someone or something throughout life. We *must* have the validity of another person.

The tendency to rely on the perceptions of others seems always at the ready despite our best intentions, hard work and even accomplishments toward independence. I was struck by this one winter when I was visiting a friend in Mexico. I have done a fair amount of traveling by myself and although I am a little anxious at the beginning, and have to fight deep beliefs that I will never be able to manage on my own, learn the currency, communicate and what not, I do, and I have done it quite adequately. But this time I met my friend at his home and for the next several days we were together, walking on the beach, talking, traveling around on public transportation and in cabs. My friend took care of all the money transactions, and I straightened it out with him later. One night we went to town to have dinner with some of his friends. After dinner, when we were calculating our respective parts of the bill, I asked my friend how many dollars I owed. One of the others looked at me and said, "You're in Mexico, you know."

I realized by that remark how dependent I had allowed myself to become while traveling with my friend. If I had been alone I would have learned the currency and enough Spanish by this time to flirt with the waitresses. But with him I became a dependent child counting on a "parent" to take care of business. He was polite enough to do it, but it could not have been fun for him either. I was astounded at how quickly I was willing to drop my own take on the world for his. I suggested we spend the next day apart, and I went to town by myself, negotiating the written and unwritten rules of riding public transportation and just getting along in this quaint Mexican town. By dinner that night I had caught up and was holding my own. I was able to separate again from my self-created mother-surrogate and re-connect with the Other Power both within and without.

Psychotherapy can be divided into broad categories with respect to the locus of the intrapsychic initiator of change. One set of orientations emphasizes the conscious, goal-directed, "willful" behavior of the person. This approach actually includes some strange bedfellows. Psychoanalysis, for example, teaches that "insight," the proper understanding of the relationship between cause and effect as a result of the "return" of the repressed will "lead" a person to change his behavior. This implies that there is no psychic event in between the insight and the behavior. Ironically, behavior therapy, cognitive therapy, and even certain inspirational approaches share with psychoanalysis the outlook that once something happens, whether it is insight, conditioning, "correct" reasoning or motivation, that behavior "changes." But it often doesn't.

The other broad category of approaches includes those that believe implicitly or explicitly, that the person changes by "releasing" certain ways of "holding," whether that holding is to people, events, behavior, perceptions, ways of thought, beliefs, or chronic affects. The release is not a conscious, goal-directed thing, but rather occurs from a part of the person not ordinarily addressed by the above approaches. My point of view is that it is the spirit rather than will which is appealed to. That appeal is made largely through the encouragement *to be aware.*

To observe, to focus clearly on exactly what is happening is a psychologically separated act in itself. The minute we do that we are in charge of our life. Even if we experience pain, it is *our* pain we are experiencing. Although suffering, we have ourselves. Noticing our behavior and inner processes interferes with the free reign we permit the demons when we operate automatically and unthinkingly. Just by noticing the randomness of our thought processes, the inconsistencies, the irrationalities, the confusion, the pain, the grief, we are reclaiming our lives. That awareness in itself activates spirit. We begin ever so subtly to move in the direction of self-regard. Changes begin immediately just by the determination to notice our lives. It is amazing. We begin to discover that we have unwittingly turned our lives and destinies over to the forces of fusion and have been, for the most part, unaware of it! We may abuse ourselves even for this, but by now, if we are lucky, we have sowed the seeds of compassion.

If a person were to spend a year doing nothing more in the way of changing himself save observing himself, his behavior and feelings and thought processes, his relations with loved ones, peers, authorities, those who rely on him—he would grow out into himself enormously. But there are ways of going about it that may intensify and broaden his opportunities to observe.

Meditation is one such way. We commit to spending a certain self-prescribed amount of time each day relaxing and noticing what goes through our mind. Our intention here is to think of nothing. We may use a mantra to help quiet and empty the mind, or we may merely attend to our breathing. We attempt to accomplish nothing but to observe. It is the ultimate example, in a way, of being a "watchman" of one's life. The results are always startling, particularly at the beginning. In contrast to the ordinary observation that I have suggested, simple "stepping outside of ourselves" to notice our life, meditation is much more focused. There is no refuge in duties to be attended to or even goal-directed thought processes. In fact, the whole idea of the exercise is to empty oneself of one's thought processes. Immediately we realize that such emptying is virtually impossible! An incessant flow of chatter, some of it seemingly focused, some of it more akin to the dream or the random thinking just prior to sleep, occupies our minds. To meditate consistently enables one to face the reality that most of our waking consciousness we are out of touch with significant dimensions of our being. It is a wonderful, although occasionally upsetting, confrontation with self. And it is enormously healing both on a physiological as well as psychological level. Just this intense awareness, by itself, helps a person get on the right track. This constant awareness of where we are "off the beam" very often sets in action the correcting mechanism of spirit, and healing occurs.

Another type of structured experience that results in focused observation is, of course, our work, counseling or psychoanalysis or psychotherapy informed by psychoanalysis. Psychoanalysis, by its structure and intentions, enables a person to observe dimensions of his experience that no other approach has been able to achieve. In the first place, it is the study of the relationship between therapist and patient. It is a chance to observe *par excellence,* and to talk about it and understand it as well. The very process of talking about it and understanding can, itself, come under scrutiny and observation. It is a virtual laboratory of life. Just about all that is possible between humans happens in this laboratory. Joyce McDougall once said,

> The psychoanalytic adventure, like a love affair, requires two people. It is not an experience in which one person "analyses" another; it is the analysis of the relationship between two persons. The analyst's participation, forged from his own psychic strengths and weaknesses, enables him to feel and understand something of what his patients are experiencing; at times, he identifies with them—the child as well as the adult, and the man as well as the woman in them—while at other moments he finds himself experiencing the thoughts and feelings of those figures of the past who have left an indelible mark on the analysand's psychic world. His most precious guide in this diffi-

cult voyage without maps is his intimate if fragmentary acquaintance with his own psychic reality. Thus the analyst shares with his analysand an experience that is in certain ways more private, at times more intense, than his relationships with those near and dear to him." (2).

Melanie Klein has taught us that there is a constant interplay between the feelings of a child and the real or imagined feelings of the mother. The child may be angry at some real or imagined deprivations (and life itself dishes those out to us no matter how loving mother is) and projects that anger onto the mother. But this is, in itself, very frightening to the child, because of her love of and need for her mother. So she introjects it back into herself and it becomes even stronger than it was before. Her new perceptions of mother, and later on the world in general, are tainted by this internalized negative feeling. She projects again, introjects again; the process continually goes on right into adulthood, shapes our relationships with all the parental surrogates we tend to create. No wonder we have such difficulty in getting along with each other!

Good psychotherapy makes it possible to observe this process. The patient makes the therapist into a sort of "auxiliary" conscience which frees the patient from his ordinary self-imposed restraints. He is able, then, to know and communicate his "untoward" impulses in the sessions. When this happens, the direction of all the internal process move toward the therapist himself. In the negotiating of the direction of these impulses toward his therapist in true emotional contact, the person gets to take a look for the first time at his distortions in perception. The unique circumstances of the psychoanalytic situation plus the skill and presence of the analyst make this possible (on a good day!) and the patient gets to understand these distortions by seeing the discrepancy between his feelings and beliefs toward the analyst and how the analyst actually is and behaves.

Classical analysis attributes this change, in the main, to the "interpretation." I tend to think that the same deep, inner process of spirit that we have described above is the actual mutative principle. But in any case, psychoanalysis provides a profound opportunity to observe just who we are and how we function and learn of the ways we have developed to survive that have resulted in the abdication of self. It can be one of the most beautiful and uniquely healing of all human relationships. Even "interpretation," *the* agency of change in the psychoanalytic technique of psychotherapy, can be understood as observation and experience of oneself found nowhere else in life.

There are many ways that we may take a good look at ourselves, from the most casual to the most structured. It is a fascinating adventure. As we do, we will notice the omnipresent human plague, the scourge of all of us: unrelenting self-criticism and abuse. And so the third and final and most important leg of the triumvirate of growing out into ourselves, that which completes intention and observation, is radical self-acceptance.

Radical Self-Acceptance

What we are about to discuss may be the most important factor in our very existence. Life is about this—just how much we love ourselves. If we love and enjoy ourselves, we are free and are living life to its fullest; if we don't love ourselves, we are being deprived of the most important thing in the history of our universe, the enjoyment of our life. As we have seen, we all suffer shame, and most of us don't know the half of it. The demons of shame lurk always in the shadows of our psyche, ready to remind us that we are no good, that there is something essentially off about us. Not that we are just limited, faulted, imperfect—but damaged; damaged goods that in some fashion should not have been allowed to be born. We differ in the amount of such suffering each of us is prone to, both the inter-personally experienced and the existential kind, but we all have this tendency.

No one escapes. And in tragic circumstances most of us are emotionally bowled over. This is no criticism. This is our nature.

On September 15, 2001, I met with a woman who was trembling and fighting back tears. "I can't go back there," she said to the air. Lilian is a nurse who had been working around the clock since the attack on the World Trade Center. "I can't look at another body part. I just saw a finger in a plastic bag." She sobbed a little. "And I can't find my sister. She was on the 101st floor of tower one, and I haven't heard from her." Now she sobbed more fully, but she still struggled to remain controlled.

In the hours she was not at the hospital, Lilian was searching the web or trudging from hospital to hospital, from one staging area to another looking for information and posting flyers about her older sister, Sandra. She estimated that she had had a total of seven hours sleep in the past four days.

We spent two hours together. One of my goals was to get her to go home and rest. "I can't; maybe there's something I could do that I would miss if I slept. My mother and my sister's daughter are bugging me to find her. I won't get any rest at home." I reflected that she would feel responsible if Sandra didn't make it and she didn't keep looking. "I know it's crazy but I keep thinking that if I had been there with her I could have made her run faster; I could have gotten her out." She relaxed into her sobs.

I counseled Lilian to not let the terrorists have another victory by yielding to her crazy thoughts. She was not crazy, I told her, but the thoughts that she was responsible or remiss in any way are crazy thoughts. I told her that when she had such a crazy thought that she should say to herself, "this a crazy thought. AND IT IS NOT HELPFUL". Such a thought hinders her search for her sister, her help to her family and her help for herself. I was trying to help her connect with that part of herself that *was* herself, that generally stood up for herself, that even argued with her sister on occasion (which we laughed about at one point). I told her to think of what she would say to a friend who had such a thought under the circumstances. She smiled, and said, "You tricked me." Lilian promised to go home and rest. An hour later I saw her on the corner handing out flyers with a picture of her sister.

Lilian's tragedy exposes the psychic vulnerability to shame that all humans are prey to. She is giving her maximum because that is the person she is. She is simultaneously driven by the love for her sister and care for her sister's daughter, not to mention the anguish of Lilian's and Sandra's mother. And when the impossibility of the task begins to overwhelm her, when to keep on going feels hopeless and stopping feels like betrayal, Lilian attacks herself. This is what we are up against when we try to encourage self-love and acceptance. The horror of the tragedy and the unthinkable pain at her loss causes a collapse of her self, her capacity to care for herself. This is the nature of severe psychological trauma. Who could escape this? The help Lilian will need, for some time, will be to help put her back in her own corner, to restore her dedication to herself, even when others are suffering and dying, even—especially—when she is absolutely powerless to do anything for them.

The horror of Lilian's story is infinitely greater than what most of us deal with each day. Yet it is the very horror of it that lays bare what each of us is vulnerable to all the time. *It is the peculiar curse of human nature that we so easily fall into feelings of shame and suffering. This is the cause of most human unhappiness. The remedy for this tendency of ours is what I call radical self-acceptance.* Without this no change is possible. This is why Lilian cannot change her behavior in the eye of the hurricane. And, in a less dramatic way, it is why we cannot change ours. For the third and perhaps the most crucial element in change is radical self-acceptance.

What I mean by self-acceptance is the gradual appreciation by a person that he is all right just the way he is; indeed he could not be other than he is at this moment. Does this mean he could never change? Of course not, although the ways that he attempts to change may be faulty and self-damaging. He is all right (he accepts himself) because he understands that he is a faulted, limited human being who can never be perfect. He may form the intention to change a particular behavior. He may observe how this behavior operates in his life. But where he stands with it this very moment is just that. And I encourage him to accept that. What's more I let him know that he is destined to stumble over shame and make mistakes until the end of his days.

What is NOT self-acceptance is the extremes of self-regard. Narcissism, of which we have spoken so much, and painful self-loathing, its underground expression, and all the gradations between these two extremes, including self-indulgence, are not what we are talking about here. As a matter of fact, narcissism and self-loathing and self-indulgence are really resistances to simple self-acceptance. Self-acceptance understands that we are not great or horrid but just average; frail and sometimes glorious creatures. It knows that no one is superior to another. Each of us is a frail person. Both ends of the self-centered spectrum are self-indulgent and grandiose. Sadly, many of us confuse those states with self-acceptance. We fear that if we are not beating up on ourselves we are self-indulgent, "selfish."

The reason I call this attitude toward ourselves *radical* is to emphasize that this quality or attitude toward ourselves is not merely some boutique characteristic, a charming modesty, but rather one which is essential to the quality of our lives and to the possibility of change itself. It is also radical because of the difficulty of the task. The tendency toward shame and irrational self-blame is so pervasive that to relinquish it somewhat demands a profound shift, a very *conversion* of our inner psychic makeup, a radical realignment of shame management within us. Narcissism and self-loathing and even violence are typical attempts to cope with shame. I offer radical self-acceptance as an antidote. Shame is a radical enemy. It demands a radical resolution.

Being out of touch with just how wonderful we are in our very ordinariness is double trouble. It keeps us from truth, and it keeps us from joy. Yet, there is an almost demonic force in us that works full time to do just that. We don't need to join that demon! Distance yourself from it. We may not be able to stop its operation just yet, but we can make a *decision* this very moment to have mercy on ourselves. We can make the decision to know that this self-criticism is a delusion, part of the human condition, not your fault, and you can form the intention this very moment to begin to let it go, or at least, to stay in your corner during the storm. By making such a decision—which you can do regardless of your psychological state—you open the door to radical self-acceptance, which does not have to do with how you feel emotionally, but rather with your commitment and fidelity to yourself. You affirm that you will be your friend regardless of what you have to go through. Even depressed and raging against yourself, there is a part of you that is determined to fight, to be loyal to your precious self.

Since shame is the source of most of our suffering, to be happy we need to learn to manage it. Since we are hard wired to experience shame, we can't avoid it entirely, but there are things we can do. We can observe, form good intentions, and we can gently and firmly remain in our corner when the self-attack occurs. We can name it rather than join it; we can face it down. Soon serenity will return, but once shame has been triggered, it will take awhile to subside, like adrenaline running in your bloodstream when there is no longer danger or when we have identified the danger as fraudulent. The release from this shame over time by refusing to join it is radical self-acceptance. It does not mean that we are always happy or free from suffering thoughts or behavior. It means we always stand in support of ourselves. We never abandon ourselves. We develop ways of coping. We remain dedicated to finding the best remedies for taking care of ourselves emotionally.

One of the reasons that radical self-acceptance is so crucial is that *no change can occur without it!* We begin to grow out into ourselves to the extent that we begin to love ourselves better. Loving ourselves does not always mean a rosy glow. On occasion, it is more like the love that we sometimes direct at our children. We can be furious with them and at the same time be thoroughly committed to help and protect them. We do for them whatever they might need to grow and prosper, even if we are not *feeling* loving at the moment.

Change never occurs when we disrespect ourselves. Remember, in the Alexander technique, the position of the head was the "primary factor" in the body's realignment? In human growth or return to spirit, radical self-acceptance is the primary agent. In fact radical self-acceptance is the primary autonomous act, the most profound psychological separation step of all. It implies two irreducible psychic events: the conviction that you are enough just as you are and the insistence that the evaluation of yourself is yours and yours alone to make.

No change can occur without acceptance, at least the way I use the word acceptance. The psychological and spiritual literature is filled with references to acceptance, self-regard, good self-concept, healthy narcissism, healthy self-love. I use the term *radical* when I refer to self-acceptance because I mean an attitude that surpasses or transcends the ordinary uses of the term. It is beyond evaluation. It is the commitment to acceptance of ourselves *just because we are ourselves and we are alive.* And we can do it even if we are suffering terribly at the moment.

Ideally, acceptance means "to receive willingly," to accept completely any particular characteristic or behavior. It is a receiving of ourselves, a witnessing, completely without judgment. We may be curious, or even charmed or shocked but never condemning. We may modify our behavior because of the demands of reality. But our basic nature we accept as a given. We are neutral. Second, we love ourselves *as a decision*, much as you might love another. Loving is really more a function of our capacity to love than of the attractiveness of the beloved. This is true of love of ourselves as well. We love ourselves because we choose to, not because we are any particular way. Loving ourselves radically and unconditionally has nothing to do with our worth—as if there is such a thing as worth. We are worthy, as a rose is worthy, because it is life and as such it is beautiful. Radical self-acceptance is the total love of oneself that transcends even unconditional positive regard or a "wonderful" evaluation of oneself. It is totally without evaluation. It accepts what is and knows that it is good. It is a hurrah, a salute to life. In loving ourselves with no strings attached, fully and without reservations, we need not be anything in particular except *capable* of full, complete, unencumbered love and rejecting of shame. And as we love, we deepen our relationship with ourselves. When we beat ourselves up, we are in relationship to a negative parental image. We are fused. To *radically* love ourselves, then, is to psychologically separate, to be free. This is why it scares us so.

Radical self-acceptance and "change" may seem on first blush to be mutually exclusive. If I accept myself completely and without reservation, why would I want to change anything? This may be true about the fierce admonitions to change that we generally direct at ourselves. Radical self-acceptance and fierceness can not coexist. But there is a gentle urge to change that does not come from a sense of something being wrong with self but rather from a spirit message that tells us that there is more for us to be, more for us to enjoy. It is not so much a desire to change as much as an intention to be more of who we are. Actually, only truly self-accepting persons will refuse to tolerate hurtful behavior in themselves. Self-criticism and judgmental evaluation actually are more likely to prompt hurtful behavior, while radical self-acceptance, eschewing fierce change, paradoxically generates growth more than anything else. Little by little, no behavior is tolerated that leads to discomfort. And no intended change will occur *deeply* without radical self-acceptance. Often the most troubling behavior, when deeply accepted by us, when shame has been transcended, when all aspiration to change it has been abandoned, changes "behind our backs."

As in all intentions, we must be humble in our aspirations. We may not really know what is good for us. And sometimes what we consciously wish to change may be behaviors that are old friends who have served us well. Sometimes we grow beyond a person who has been our friend and we must move on. We do this, hopefully, with consideration and tenderness, mindful of the sensibilities of the other. So, too, with aspects of ourselves that we want changed. It may take a long time. We need to be patient and avoid grandiose expectations, for they stem from fusion with mother. We are what we are, and at any moment that is a function of the conflict between spirit and demons. Radical self-acceptance is the ultimate psychological separation, the spiritual act of knowing we are all right just the way we are.

But the intention to free ourselves from the negative influence of our early caretakers does involve commitment, constant examination of our intentions, vigilant observation and, of course, unrelenting attempts at radical self-acceptance, the determination to be always on our side, even when depressed. We must be ever mindful of ways to countermand the propagandizing with which we daily must contend, both from inside and out. We need to find nurturing rather than toxic relationships and foster them. We need to find structures in our lives—groups, societies, synagogues—that provide encouragement, acceptance, and nurture. To stay alone is to stay with mother. We need to affirm ourselves each day in ways that make sense to us and that work. *We must tell ourselves each day that we love ourselves.* We must say NO! to old behaviors that have consistently hurt us. True courage is not jumping out of a foxhole and attacking the machine gun nest. True courage is saying no to a piece of cake when we are trying to lose weight. True courage is any step—and it is generally the small ones that are the most important—that goes against deeply ingrained parental imperatives and injunctions. And it is also the immediate forgiveness of ourselves when we miss the mark, for sometimes we *will* miss the mark.

Change or growth or development in personality comes not so much from doing the hard things but rather in relentlessly doing that which is doable. As the wonderful old philosopher Mae West put it, "I never yield to temptation unless I have to." The trick is in courageously resisting temptation *when we can*. Sometimes attempting to do the impossible is actually engaging in the battle of wills. It is assaulting the demons with ego, but you can never win because ego is part of the demons! This is not the way of spirit. The way of spirit is to surrender ego to spirit and acknowledge our powerlessness in dealing with the demons. That surrender and acknowledgment of powerlessness neutralizes the demons and strengthens the spirit and gradually over time the task becomes easier. When the task is easier it is the time for it to be done. And this requires humility and patience and cooperation.

But the most powerful agent in the development of radical self-acceptance is the emotional contact between patient and therapist. True emotional contact always elicits radical self-acceptance. Think of the moments of beautiful contact you have with a friend or relative or lover. When each brings himself to the other in presence and receptivity, the true emotional contact that results is one of joy and complete self and mutual acceptance. What makes it *true* is the honesty of the emotional availability of each to the other. What makes it *emotional* is not necessarily a display of emotionality between the two, though there is nothing wrong with that, but rather the availability of their emotion to themselves! This is what happens over time in the true emotional contact of patient and therapist, regardless of the subject matter of their inquiry at any particular time and regardless of the limitations in the sharing of personal information by the therapist. And as time moves on, the quality of radical self-acceptance that is increasingly enjoyed in therapy gets transferred into the patient's relationship with himself. He becomes more frequently in true emotional contact with himself. Radical self-acceptance is no longer just an intention, it is also a way of life. And even though he may be battered by his residual neurosis, and shame may still be elicited, as he negotiates these states there will be a steady continuing self-respect and serenity. He will resolve guilt; he will step outside of shame and this will continue after therapy stops. Even when suffering, he will be capable of peace.

Like everyone, I have been struggling with these matters since I was a boy. No one ever entirely frees himself from these struggles. We never complete the task. We need to completely accept this as well. I have decided to forgive God the divine mystery and my limitations and to have fun, to be happy. I have decided to intend to have an "easy life:" to keep on gently observing, form good intentions, diligently eschew disdain and pray for absolute acceptance of myself and others. I consistently reinforce this prayer by true emotional contact with others. I then try to do whatever needs to be done, (not always so easy), trying to keep well below my perfectionism and just a notch above my sloth. Yes, there *is* work to do. Wresting the spirit back and chancing the new in the midst of an eternity of influences is our task. I need all the help I can get. But all the pain and suffering in the world, all the loss and grief, all the hurt, is made sustainable by those moments when I make true emotional contact with another, and, together, we deeply and intrinsically know that we are just the way we are supposed to be.

Summary

1. Change happens by itself when the right conditions are created. Don't try to force it.

2. The beginning (and constant companion) of all change is radical self-acceptance.

3. Most change occurs in the context of intention, observation, and radical self-acceptance.

4. Intentions are crucial, must be made clear, but must always be tentative. We don't always know what is good for us, at least on the conscious level, and have to monitor this carefully. Accepting where we are at the present and observing is often the most efficient approach.

5. Observation is crucial because we are encrusted with psychic habits developed over what is experienced as centuries of psychological struggle. Observation, plus other powerful methods such as meditation and psychoanalysis, help us to see just how we work, inside and out.

6. We are working against centuries of propagandizing and we must develop powerful tools of self-propaganda to combat these influences on a daily basis. We must take responsibility for loving ourselves and seeking out in our environment people and situations that are nurturing. This is a daily obligation.

7. Fully experiencing painful affects in the context of true emotional contact evaporates them. We need not be afraid. No one died of a feeling.

8. No change occurs without radical self-acceptance. Radical self-acceptance does not mean that we are always happy; it does not mean that we believe ourselves to be perfect and don't have to aspire to further growth. It means, rather, that wherever we are, whatever we are experiencing, we are committed to ourselves; we are our friends, even if we don't feel loving at the moment. We must help our clients form this intention, right from the beginning.

9. As time moves on, the true emotional contact between client and counselor will result in a deepening of the client's radical self-acceptance, a conversion, so to speak, from a mere intention to a deep friendship with one's self. This will continue throughout life. The precious relationship between client and counselor is replaced by the special relationship between the client and himself. This is the wonderful result of his therapeutic work and our greatest gift to him.

Notes

(1) Levine, S. Who Dies? An investigation of conscious living and conscious dying (Basic Books, 1982)
(2) McDougall, J. Plea for a Measure of Abnormality (New York: International University Press, 1980)

6

Thunder and Gossamer: The Story of Sarah

In January 1991 I received this letter:

Dear Jim:

This late Christmas card comes to you from Sarah Maloney—with best wishes, and apologies for having fallen out of touch. I hope it finds you *well*.

In a sentence, things finally worked out for me the way that *you* convinced me was possible. I got married to someone who loves me for myself, and takes care of me and my old Dad, and supports my art. He's Ted Larson, the guy I spoke to you about in our last couple of sessions. He's now a college English Professor (he's a few years older than me) who lives here in Western Maryland and teaches at a small college across the Potomac in West Virginia. We've got all the same values and interests. My health is *much* better (no smoking!), and I'm now living a normal life (driving a car, etc., etc.), as well as continuing with my art—and starting to get some money and recognition for it, at long last! Put my new name and address in your Rolodex; I'll schedule a visit with you next time we're in New York.

Thanks for everything!! Thanks for believing in me.

Sarah

(address and phone)

I was stunned. I hadn't heard from Sarah since the fall of 1987 when I called her to see how she was doing. She had stopped coming to therapy the previous year, rather abruptly. She was experiencing increasing financial difficulties, she explained, and felt she could no longer manage to pay for treatment. While I believed she had made considerable gains, at the time she terminated she was living alone in a studio apartment in the Chelsea section of Manhattan's West Side, living on what little her aging and retired father was able to send her and some moneys from the occasional sale of a painting.

Sarah is an amazing artist, an enormously gifted woman who was in the stranglehold of a crushing depression when she first came to see me in the Summer of 1980—a beautiful young woman of 24 with long golden hair. She walked in a sort of glide and spoke so gently that it took enormous concentration to hear her words. She was like gossamer. Her visit to me that summer and a rare dinner with Maria, a friend of hers and a patient of the colleague who referred Sarah to me, were the only times she had left her apartment—or her bed—in months. When last I saw her in 1986, she had gotten to the point of working again, freeing herself from some abusive situations with men, starting to socialize with both men and women. She was determined to free herself from financial dependency on her father, a retired librarian, widowed, who lived in the family home in Virginia, almost as a recluse. His contact with reality was, in some sense, "taking care of Sarah."

She told me during that phone conversation that she was doing well, going out more, working and dating. She told me she would like to resume therapy, but was just getting on her feet financially, and could not afford it. She would call when things improved. It was good to hear that she was doing OK, but I believed that her work was not complete and had hoped that she would return to treatment. I was troubled at the "loose ends" of her life and the rather abrupt ending of the treatment. Also, it had occurred at a time of personal difficulty in my life, and I was feeling guilty. Had I, in some way, failed her? She seemed so alone in life. And she had worked so hard in her therapy. I had extensive notes of our work together and I took them out and began to review them. It was during my work with Sarah that my appreciation of mother-fusion deepened. For Sarah came from a family dedicated to enmeshment, and Sarah had shown me the results of these experiences as well as the possibilities of disentangling oneself from the myriad connections to one's caretakers through true contact. It was Sarah who coined the word, "marbleizing." As we painstakingly examined the "strands" of connections to the "familial mass" she came from, she had the visual image of a piece of beef. Each strand was like gristle and separating oneself from the undifferentiated mass was like pulling a piece of gristle from the beef. In therapy, on a good day, whole chunks would come out. Most of the time it was painstaking work, strand by strand.

Virginia

Sarah was born in suburban Virginia (details, of course, disguised), the second of two children, both girls. Her parents were different than the rest of the community. They didn't have a car, for one thing. Shopping was done by walking the few blocks to a neighborhood delicatessen or taking a bus to the supermarket, making the trip home with arms laden down with packages for all the community to see. Sarah remembers being inconvenienced by this state of affairs as well as deeply embarrassed. There was nothing she could do to influence her parents to purchase a car.

> We would all stand at the bus stop, my parents, Joannie and me, arms filled with packages. I was mortified. As a teenager, and even before, we were the odd balls. I was terrified that one of my friends would drive by and see us. As a result of experiences like these I always felt strange, different. Even when I was away from my family and with my friends there was this lingering feeling that I was an odd ball.

She described her mother as the more "normal" of her parents. Mother could be sociable and participate in friendly interaction with neighbors. At times she was even bright and cheery. Sarah recalls that what little joy and fun she had at home as a child was with her mother. Her father, on the other hand, was withdrawn and isolated. Raised by three maiden aunts, he was virtually a recluse. When he returned (by public transportation!) from his librarian's job, he would lower the shades and cut off all interaction with the outside world. He cut off contact with the inside world of feelings as well. He brooked little expression of affect. Anger and signs of sexuality were unacceptable and punishable, as you shall see, by total rejection. The children were encouraged to be friendly and pleasant, to have friends and play, above all to do what would bring approval upon the family. But they were not to stay over at the homes of playmates. No neighborhood children were allowed into the Maloney household.

From as far back as she can remember, Sarah was told that her family was essential to her well being. Without them there was no one you could trust. It was all right for children to have friends—friends are *for* children—playmates, not intimates. But real emotional contacts outside the family were constantly denigrated. This was a powerful message and one which plagued Sarah. When I met her she had a romantic involvement with a young man, Ramon, which she felt she had to keep hidden from her family. He was culturally different and they would not approve, but the problem was much deeper than that. Once she reported:

> I spoke to my father about Ramon. First I felt guilt, then anger at feeling guilt, then for a short while depressed. *I have a strong feeling that my family is more important than anyone else. I was experiencing guilt that I had allowed an "outsider" to become important to me. I was taught that people (my friends) meant nothing to me and that I meant nothing to them.*

She went on:

I knew that the first was untrue, but the second part I believed and still believe—which, by the way, leads to a lot of insecurity in my relationships; I reach the panic point when I realize that I am beginning to care about someone.

Later in that session she wondered if this belief didn't turn into a self-fulfilling prophecy, serving to prove that what her parents told her is true.

Attempts at relationships have left me feeling like the prodigal son. Yet there was a contradiction in my parents' attitude: they treated me as if I was the most important person on the face of the earth—but others could not and would not see how wonderful I was, and therefore I should have nothing to do with them. This has led to a contradiction in me, but I honestly do believe that I am a good, worthy person.

As a youngster, prior to adolescence, Sarah was an outgoing "tomboy," full of adventure and liveliness. She had many friends, boys and girls. She did well in school. Her relationship with her older sister, while somewhat distant, was not overtly troubled. Her father was remote, but not unfriendly. She describes her relationship with her mother as very close. While she was allowed to interact with the other children, her mother preferred that she play only with her sister. But Sarah's perception was that her sister was hostile and in alliance with her father against her liveliness. When she spoke of these perceptions, tentatively, to her mother, Mother denied it.

It was very hard for me to know something my mother did-n't approve of. Although my mother could be fun and happy she showed signs of depression early in my life, and I felt her depression to be intimately connected with me. When I was pleasing her, she was happy. When I was doing something she didn't approve of—like spending "too much" time with my playmates, away from the family, or when I saw something or understood something differently than her, she would become depressed. *It seemed my mother's happiness was in my hands.*

Alice Miller, in her profound and moving discussion of the "Drama of the Gifted Child" (1) reports her experiences of persons similar to Sarah whom she analyzed.

> In my work with all these people, I found that every one of them has a childhood history that seems significant to me.
> - There was a *mother* who at the core was emotionally insecure, and who depended for her narcissistic equilibrium on the child behaving, or acting, in a particular way. This mother was able to hide her insecurity from the child and from everyone else behind a hard, authoritarian, and even totalitarian facade.
> - This child had an amazing ability to perceive and respond intuitively, that is, unconsciously, to this need of the mother, or of both parents, for him to take on the role that had unconsciously been assigned to him.
> - This role secured "love" for the child—that is, his parents' narcissistic cathexis. He could sense that he was needed and this, he felt, guaranteed him a measure of existential security.

This was strikingly the case with Sarah. Yet she had this remarkable spirit—the tomboy in her was an expression of it—and she was capable of happy and related engagement with the world, even though it was not really appreciated or encouraged by her parents. There was a thin corridor of "childhood" play that was allowed her but little response to her idiosyncratic needs. Any personal expression of self—impulse, sensation, ideas, motor expression—in essence, any expression of *unique self* was discouraged.

Early on, then, Sarah was in deep conflict between the expression of herself and her "obligation" to take care of her emotionally needy parents. The father was clearly in distress. The mother could present a positive, happy façade, which Sarah fiercely wanted to believe, but mother was, in reality, very insecure. In addition she suffered from severe depression and then, if Sarah had any chance at all, Mother became seriously ill. The messages Sarah was constantly getting left her with a *deep belief* that she was responsible for mother's illness. There developed in this otherwise healthy and feisty little girl, the seeds of profound depression and the fusion of her behavior and affect with the affect and vicissitudes of the lives of her parents.

As her life progressed, she was sometimes happy and successful and energetic and accomplishing, but mostly depressed and withdrawn, emotionally isolated. A childhood dream:

> I am running with a group of children; I feel normal but I keep falling down. I can't keep up with the other children. We are running in a grassy field. The dream is in color; my senses are still normal.

It was not that her parents set about causing their daughter difficulty. Actually, there was a great deal of love among the four of them. It was just that her parents were so needy themselves, had been so emotionally neglected in their own childhood, that the sadly human tendency to make their children the solution to their lifelong quest to be seen, themselves, resulted in damaging and relentless anti-spirit propagandizing. And from a source, the most powerful she would ever encounter, Mother.

Sarah once made a chronological chart of the course of her illness throughout her life:

Up until 8	not depressed
9-12	mildly depressed
12-15	severely depressed
16-18	fluctuated among all three but with the longest normal periods

19-21	fluctuated among all three but periods of depression becoming longer and more severe
22-23	depressed nearly all the time
23-24	depression varies from moderate to severe with physical symptoms beginning to reappear
25-	severely depressed

Initially, Sarah told me she was a happy child. She reported periods of great happiness with her mother. As time went on, in our work, she began to see things differently. Once, in discussing her father's current denial of her plight, she said, "He has to begin to acknowledge how disturbed I was as a child. I was a gifted, but disturbed child." Finally, as she got well and began to reclaim the feelings she had abandoned in her childhood, she told me, "a depressed child is deprived of all the feelings of childhood."

At the end of her childhood dream she remarked, "My senses are still normal." This is a dramatically important observation. While part of her was a typical "kid" Sarah was aware very early that something was "wrong" and, as is typical with children, she was alone in this awareness. She lived in a world—her family—where questions were always deflected or not noticed. In fact there was a marked "not noticing" of behavior and physical and emotional states that were emotionally "threatening" in some way, or did not fit into the family belief system. Thus, if Sarah was markedly depressed, and this delayed the beginnings of her sexual expression, that was just fine with her father. The lack of attention to her physical condition bordered on neglect. When she began psychotherapy she was in dire need of major therapeutic orthodontics. (This serious neglect of physical problems is not uncommon in psychologically fused families. The belief system is so self-centered and fearful that it often interferes with the appropriate perception of reality and consequent appropriate action. On several occasions Sarah's mother was denied medical attention even at the point of death. *The irony in this tragic way of dealing with the world is that the unseparated conviction that only the family can be trusted often places one in jeopardy. Those who foster fusion are generally the most self-centered and therefore unreliable people. Psychological fusion is a deadly game!)*

The blinds were closed on Sarah's emotional life as well as in the house where she lived. Her mother seems to have recognized Sarah's emotional and spiritual beauty, but was so troubled herself that she was unable to avoid fusing with her. Sarah knew that she was loved and appreciated. She maintained, as I mentioned above, that this resulted in a belief inside of herself that, despite all her pain and trouble, she was a good person. While there is some truth to this belief, it also made her protect her mother's memory and interfered with Sarah's fully appreciating the spot she was in. We had to struggle with this, painstakingly, in our work. For it is in truly understanding our life with our parents that we have a chance to give room to our spirit.

Her sister was the only person with whom her parents approved of her making contact. Each had different roles in the family. Joannie was allowed to be angry and expressive but Sarah was not. When her sister caused "trouble," Sarah had to be especially "good" to counteract her mother's depressive response. Anger was not allowed Sarah at any time. Nor could she get away.

Somewhere inside her she connected her desire to become a unique person with her mother's depression. When she was 12, her mother's brother died, and mother became extremely depressed. "His death brought about the only separation from my mother before her illness. On the day that my mother left I became violently ill with a stomach flu. I remember my father being nice to me then." Sarah remained in a severe depression, herself, for several years. That summer she built an elaborate doll's house in the basement of her home. She would spend hours alone in the cool dark absorbed in this activity. When I knew her she still dreaded the onset of summer. It always seemed to evoke this time of pain and extreme loneliness for her.

Her world became solitary and confusing. When she played with friends she was self-conscious. She "knew" she was different, because she saw her family's idiosyncrasies. As she played with her friends there was also the constant voice of her parents cautioning against making contact with "outsiders." At home she felt guilty because she did, indeed, have feelings for her friends. She even had good times with them, and she had to keep that truth hidden. There was no place in her life just to be herself.

Physical illness was a powerful factor in her childhood. Her mother had a bout with rheumatic heart disease when Sarah was seven. She identified the onset of her own depression with the idea that it was her own liveliness and expressiveness that resulted in mother's not being well. Sarah also believed that her resentment toward her father for not having a car (which precluded her visiting friends and relatives who lived in different places) precipitated his rejection of her. She was only eight years of age at the time, but she began to conclude that *her feelings and behavior had profound and unchangeable impact on her parents*. They could make her mother "sick"; they *made* her father strange and rejecting. She responded to all of this with depression. She also noticed that her own illnesses got her some attention. Once she told me, "I made myself sick so that they would take care of me."

Sarah became convinced that emotions were dangerous. When she felt happy her parents withdrew or got sick. Feeling good and behaving effectively led to separation. At the time of her uncle's death, for example, when mother "left her" and she subsequently became depressed, Sarah had actually been feeling quite well and was cautiously easing herself into adolescence. And then this happens! Feeling too good leads to loss. Being depressed and sick kept you close to your loved ones whom you could "count on." To be happy was to be "bad"; to suffer was to be "good."

On the other hand, it *was* permissible to be happy with mother. "I was depressed with nearly everyone except my mother and I strongly suspect that she was depressed with nearly everyone except me." Another time she told me, "the times that I spent with my mother were the happiest of my childhood; that is why it is so painful to me to remember them." What she did not realize, as she told me this, was that she was really describing "fusion," the sense of security and bliss accompanying the approval of the mothering one. She did not realize, either, that all her suffering also involved her "oneness" with mother. And there was a lot more of that. The price for that fusion, which made her feel safe and even happy sometimes, was the deep belief that autonomous, separated spirit-based behavior and feelings and thinking were destructive to her parents; to engage in this made her "bad." Depression was the appropriate mood for this "badness." She was later to discover her central deep belief, her "main idea," buried so deep that it would take years to become conscious: She *must* be one with mother to be good, even if it meant suffering, even if it meant death.

Sarah is an extremely intelligent and creative person but her thought processes were riddled with injunctions. The first was against thinking, itself. One of the major characteristics of depression is the inability to think effectively. So she often was unable to think clearly. Then there were the *Deep Beliefs*.

The overall one, of course, insinuated that she was not enough in herself. Her welfare depended on her being fused with her family. She was constantly mindful of what her mother would think, or of the effect her behavior, feelings, and even thought would have on her mother and, by extension, her father and sister.

There were other deep beliefs, corollaries of the principal one. These were not always conscious, nor did they always control her behavior. But they were always lurking. She believed there were repercussions for her free, spontaneous, "spirited" behavior. To dance to her own tune, soon enough she would pay the piper. These Deep Beliefs prohibited autonomous, independent, separated behavior. All aspects of her life were affected. Sarah's sexuality, her creativity, her productivity, her friendships, her physical environment, her very person—nothing escaped the taint of fusion.

Nonetheless, Sarah made a remarkable surge forward. She decided to come to New York City to study art. This was stunning for several reasons. To begin with, she was slated to attend her mother's college. Leaving home was begrudgingly conceded if mother and Sarah could share *Alma Mater*. She was accepted and ready to go. But Sarah lobbied for art school—not just majoring in art in a good college—but art School, specifically the Art Students League in New York City, a famous center enjoying an outstanding reputation. It was known also for the Bohemian life style of its students and faculty, and it was right in the center of a major den of iniquity, New York City. Her parents let her apply only because they didn't think that she had a chance of acceptance. Sarah won a scholarship. She was among a handful of students selected in a nationwide competition of high school artists.

Her parents did not want her to go. They predicted she would be unhappy, out of place and even in jeopardy in New York. Sarah summoned up courage, and her spirit prevailed. She stepped out of the enmeshment of her family and suburban Virginia for Manhattan. And she was ecstatic.

Despite all the conflicts Sarah experienced and all the propagandizing she was subject to and all the Deep Beliefs she had developed, her spirit kept her surging forward. Her art was a prime example of this. She was an artist and she knew it. She also had real contact with friends, boys and girls; these were the nucleus of her capacity to form healthy and abundant relationships. Throughout the painful period of withdrawal and isolation which was to come, this capacity for love would never abandon her.

The summer before she was to go to New York was a heady one. She had a relationship with a young man of color who was more sophisticated than her average schoolmates. There were parties and moonlight drives. Sarah had always been terrified of sex. The idea of being intimate with someone, of showing her flawed nakedness to a fellow human being, boggled her mind. Yet there were tentative forays. She felt alive and strong despite her parents' attempt at sabotage. When trouble developed with her boyfriend, mother said, "good, you're well rid of him." After a brief period of communication with Sarah, just after her prize was announced, Father again withdrew. Her sister was engaged to be married and ignored her. Yet, she was full of hope and promise and peer friendship and romance. For the only time in their lives Sarah and her mother were not speaking as she left for New York. "We were at each others "throats," said Sarah.

New York

So at 17 years of age Sarah Maloney came to New York City. She was wide-eyed and frightened and deliriously happy. She felt the fear of an even younger child set loose alone in the streets of a big city. She also felt the happiness of those early years in her life when she was the spontaneous happy tomboy of the neighborhood. She didn't miss home. She felt free.

She settled into the life of a young Art student in New York City. She quickly made friends, boys and girls, moved into a small apartment near school with several of them. She threw herself into her work and the heady social life of her new bohemian playmates. She dated, experimented with drugs and alcohol and sex. She even moonlighted as an artist's model for some of the classes in her school. All of a sudden there seemed to be no limitations. The first year away from home she recalls as the happiest in her life.

There was, however, an unremitting sense of guilt. She was having such a good time, yet she was not with her family. In addition she was mindful of the dysphoria of her home and of the chronic illnesses of her family, particularly her mother. Her mother was frequently ill—events Sarah associated with her "bad" behavior—and now mother had some mysterious progressive disease, later diagnosed as progressive mylofibrosis; she seemed always to be ill. There was constant pressure to go home, and for some time Sarah resisted this pressure. She made brief visits, always reverted to how she was before she left, and was glad to come back to her new life. Her spirit urged her forward into new places and ideas and friendships. It encouraged her to develop her work and set free her creativity. Her demons, at the same time, constantly prodded her to return to the old ways. These demons incarnated in guilt and worry and the chronic belief that somehow her happiness was contributing to her mother's illness. This idea was supported indirectly by her father and, less subtly, by her sister who was anxious to perpetuate Sarah's sense of guilt in order to lessen her own. She was to tell Sarah at her mother's deathbed, "Mommy was really devastated because you never came back."

For the most part, though, particularly in the first two years in New York, Sarah was alive and having a wonderful time. She learned her craft, was exposed to new ideas and techniques, received good feedback on her work, and began to get the sense that she was a gifted artist. And in the hours after work, she sat in "P.J.Carney's," a saloon around the corner from the art School, across the avenue from Carnegie Hall. There she learned about life in the steamy atmosphere of artists, students and teachers, musicians, actors, New York characters, brilliance and seediness.

She had many friends, some bizarre experiences, some love affairs. One was with a gifted Hispanic young man from an inner-city ghetto, also on scholarship. He was like no other she had known. She described him as beautiful. He was worldly wise and extremely sensitive. He was a gifted artist who also hung out in bad neighborhoods and did bad things. For his part, he was enchanted by this longhaired, blond, soft-spoken southern lady. They developed a deep friendship.

There was much mingling with the faculty at this institute, and some teachers preyed on innocent and susceptible newcomers. One such, Paul, an older man, married with children, courted Sarah. He, unsuccessfully for the most part, tried to separate her from the "pack" of students she "ran" with. Sarah was receiving much attention, professionally and personally, and was growing out into the beautiful person she is. Part of her attraction to everyone, I should mention, is the way she was with people. Sarah is a very kind and caring person. She related in a sensitive and responsive way to others. She was a giver. In addition, there was her not so healthy tendency to take responsibility for others. These are traits that people enjoy and respond to. Nor are they unnoticed by the human predators among us.

At the same time the pressure to return home was constant and increasing. Her mother's condition was worsening. Then Sarah suffered a fall while crossing the street and broke her ankle. She was housebound for a period of time and then got around only with difficulty. The family pressure to return reached a crescendo and Sarah yielded. She didn't stay long, but something began to change within her. She gradually and subtly returned to the role she played in her family. She started to become depressed again. She felt guilty for all the good times she had in New York. She became anxious at the realization that she cared for people other than those in her family, and that others seemed to care for her—something she was repeatedly propagandized against throughout her life. She began to associate her separation from her family, her newfound success, her emotional contact with others, with the deterioration in her family, particularly her mother. She returned to New York, where by now she had her own studio apartment, but gradually withdrew from her friends and yielded to the pressure from Paul, the older, married teacher, to become his lover. For the next period of time she was in his spell, largely unhappy, but fused with him.

Little by little Sarah allowed herself to be sucked back into the inner atmospheres of her early life. Although she was living in New York, physically away from her parents, emotionally she was in the process of re-creating her early life, being subsumed into chronic affects, old familiar feelings that had long dogged her. She gradually withdrew from her friends and from Ramon. She spent more and more time alone in her apartment. Initially, she blamed her isolation on work but gradually even that fell away. She waited in solitude for Paul to appear. She became an appendage to his life, hanging out in the bars that he frequented, taking his fringe friends as her own.

Ramon was distraught. She told me, "I thought he wouldn't be. I was taught people wouldn't care." But Ramon represented freedom and emotional contact, whereas Paul represented fusion with mother. Sarah said, "whenever I had an emotional feeling toward anyone I would be anxious because I wasn't supposed to feel anything toward anyone other than my family." With Paul she was safe. She had no real feelings toward him. She just felt depressed. Involvement with him became a way of giving the appearance of an independently functioning person, but, in truth, she remained in the psychological world of her family. Whenever she stood up to him, Paul would say he was getting a pain in his chest, and she would back off. This went on for two years. Her trips to Virginia became more frequent. Her mother was failing. "She always seemed to get better when I was there," said Sarah.

And then her mother died. January 1st, 1978 was the last day she saw her mother out of bed. New Year's Day had long since become a symbol of fusion with her family. It was unthinkable to spend New Year's Day with anyone but them. She always returned home for that day. No matter what was going on in her life; no matter how involved she might be in others' lives and they in hers, on New Years she came "home"—that was where the people who really cared were. For years after her mother's death, she spent this time with her father. "We would hang out in a museum and my father would comment on how all these famous artists now were dead; at home after dinner, he would reflect morbidly on death." So on this New Years Day she was home, her mother was up and about, and the family could indulge their denial of mother's state. Until the end they minimized the illness and even *in extremis*, failed to call the doctor on time.

Her mother died in March, ten years to the day after her brother's death. Sarah returned to New York, and for a short period of time, seemed to get better. She took courses at a local liberal arts college, became more involved with some of her girl friends and had a wild fling with another professor at the college. There was a brief return to drugs and alcohol. It was as if her spirit was gasping for breath. She desperately fought the impending pseudo-death of major depression, which was coming at her like fog across a field in the early morning. She did all those things she associated with the happiness and vitality of her early childhood and her recent years in New York.

But depression was not to be denied. For added to all the other reasons already suggested for her pain and self-criticism, was now an even more powerful internal rearrangement, a more insidious shift that moved her across the line from merely experiencing depression to seemingly being depression itself. She now *became* her mother, kept her alive, as it were, by yielding to her fusion with her. She kept mother alive, this way, for mother's sake, for her own, and also for the family. The family had fallen apart. Now they could relate to Sarah as if she were mother, and all could go about their business. Sister married, father working and calling Sarah every Saturday night at eleven P.M. and Sarah, literally vegetating, in her increasingly slovenly room.

She became more and more a recluse. Her basic vulnerability in life, where she was stuck, was being embedded in her parents. Although she had lived life in an apparently different way for several years, her deepest belief all this time was that to be different than her parents was a betrayal. From time to time she was able to break free, but this was bravado and easily sabotaged by the vicissitudes of life or the behavior of her parents. Her immersion in her parents was so profound that it affected every aspect of her life. She retreated into her tiny unkempt apartment. She told me once, "I couldn't fix it up because my mother always said she wanted to do it with me." She withdrew from her girlfriends because her mother never had friends. These were not reasons she was aware of at the time, but rather things that became clear to her as our work progressed. She stopped being the toy of Paul, would not be shown off by him in social situations. She replaced him with Ramon who re-entered her life, this time not the sexy star of the Art School but rather a strung-out junkie and alcoholic. The two could take some comfort in each other, neither having to fake a good impression for the other.

Her sister supported her isolation. "You're better off alone," she advised. Sarah stopped working completely. "My work habits became like my parents' life, confused and unproductive." She no longer took classes. Her life was a shambles. She could not be employed, so her father paid her rent and sent her a pittance more. She lived extremely frugally. She no longer drank or used drugs, her only expenses now being cigarettes and the occasional food and beverages she kept on hand to entertain Ramon on his intermittent visitations. She was virtually starving herself.

Sarah had come to New York excited and optimistic and confident that she would transcend the fusion of her family. She had a scholarship, friends, a wonderful school and life. She lived in "this sunny little apartment a few blocks from the river." She was beautiful and everyone loved her. The world was hers to take. Now she was a recluse in this apartment that was falling down around her. It needed repair work, but she was unable to negotiate this with her landlord. She was physically sick. She rarely went out. She had a relationship with a drug addict that by the world's standards seemed exploitative and abusive. She earned no money and lived on the little sent to her by her father who loved the control over his beautiful adult daughter. She had dropped out of school. A brilliant artist, she no longer worked. Once reveling in parties and wine and song and youthful romance—separated behaviors—she now spent most of her days sick in bed, the shades drawn in her decrepit apartment, scarcely bathing. She was only aware of profound depression. She had no feelings of her own. She had no energy. She could not think for herself. Again she was in the basement of her home in Virginia that steely summer when she built her dolls' house world in the dark by herself. Only now she never came up. And there were no dolls.

Yet she stayed in New York, resisting the incessant entreaties of her father and sister to return to Virginia where she would be taken care of and safer. "It's safer here," Sarah once told me. "I don't know why people think it's safer in the suburbs than in Manhattan; it's much more dangerous to your spirit in the suburbs; Manhattan is much safer. I would die if I went back to Virginia."

So lying in her bed in her dark, decrepit apartment, frozen still in depression, terrified and lost and bereft, Sarah reached into a part of herself, her spirit, and decided to go forward, not back. And on Bastille Day,

1980, two years and four months after her mother's death, she came into my office. It was a Wednesday at 2:15 P.M. Our work had begun, and it would continue for six years.

The Therapy

Sarah spoke so softly it was almost impossible to hear her. Her thought processes were extremely slowed down. She was aware of no emotions. This "thing" had happened to her and she had no knowledge or understanding of it, or feeling about it. When I suggested that her depression was a choice in some sense, as bizarre as that might seem, she became annoyed. She did not like that idea. Psychotherapy had begun.

When she started therapy she was deeply depressed. It would take all the effort she could muster on the day she would visit me to get out of bed and shower and groom herself. She was still interested in that, perhaps excessively so, having had it pounded into her by her mother that her currency in life was her beauty. In addition, she must avoid criticism at all costs. Her long blond hair needed special care and her neglect of it, for the most part when she was not going out or having Ramon over, made it even more difficult to manage. Even as she began to heal, her body rebelled and she experienced numerous physical symptoms including a matting of her hair which made it finally totally unmanageable. She was forced to cut it short which signaled, ironically, a dramatic shift in one of her deep beliefs about herself, viz., that she had to be a strikingly lovely, longhaired blonde beauty to minimally get by in life.

She was always preoccupied with her weight and her appearance. When I met her she was thin but not anorexic. She had been mildly anorexic as an early teenager which she later associated with her mother's beginning to lose weight at the onset of her illness. She had been told that she must be immaculate (which she always was when I saw her) and that her hair had to be perfect before she could go out. She would spend hours preparing for our sessions. Later when she was dating she would do the same. Her early fear of sex was accompanied by a conviction that her body was unacceptable. Her teeth had been badly neglected so that she needed major orthodontics. As therapy progressed, she developed a major yeast problem that she felt invaded her whole system. I was never able to determine how much of this was biologically based and how much of it was a deep contempt for her body and its functions. She was forever going to doctors and seeking out remedies. Paradoxically, the physical difficulties seemed to get worse as she got better emotionally. This is not unusual. The more one progresses in psychotherapy the deeper the level of the fusion that is manifested. Also, fear of bodily illnesses is often the last ditch strategy of the demons to get the person to abandon her spirit and "back off." Her physical problems also fed into her anxiety about meeting men and tended to keep her in limited, unsatisfactory relationships, in effect, keeping her at home.

As our work proceeded, the connection between her bodily concerns and those of her mother kept coming to the surface. Sarah had some ambivalence about being female which she felt, sometimes, to be an inconvenience. "I always have to carry something and look good. Men have it much easier." Sarah's physical troubles give witness to the most basic ways we fuse with our caretakers, even to the extent of becoming one with their biological processes. Psychological separation makes it possible for us, in some sense, to "choose" even our own biological destinies and not merely repeat that of our progenitors. Genetic predisposition is part of it, of course. But our body self is much more infiltrated by psychological factors than we ordinarily consider, as we saw with my patient Martin in chapter two.

When a person comes to therapy it is a poignant moment. There is often the feeling of failure. The truth is, it is a moment of victory. For some time, the person's spirit has been "central-to-others," to the point of moral neglect of self. If there is any failure, it is in this self-abandonment. One's spirit must always be "central-to-self," in order to play out its unique destiny. When the agony of the spirit prevented from doing this is so great, its lust for life so long betrayed that the person drags herself, in whatever condition, to a place of hope, it is a victory for the universe. Once there, however, the fused self flares up and does everything possible to betray the spirit. But at least the spirit has a chance, because now there is an ally, the therapist, devoted to that spirit.

Sarah brought great resistance to the process. This resistance represented the interpersonal manifestations of fusion with her family, particularly her mother. She displayed her inflexible and unconscious identifications with mother and all her behavior in response to her mother's injunctions, real or imagined. She was not supposed to have emotions. She was not supposed to think clearly and for herself. She was not supposed to have autonomous deep beliefs or question the ones she developed in the midst of her daily life with her family while growing. She was not supposed to have meaningful relationships with anyone other than her family. She was not supposed to love; she was not supposed to feel sexual toward a man she respected. She was not supposed to work in an autonomous, spirit-directed way. She was not supposed to establish true contact with anyone.

And so she did what each of us does in many situations and what one certainly does in psychotherapy: she transferred onto me her view of the world. She behaved toward me the way her parents would want her to, and with the behaviors they would approve of. She tried to please me in order to avoid true contact. But her spirit in its quiet way was relentless. From the bowels of her depression she began to speak, with my encouragement, and to tell her tale. She never ceased being astounded at my acceptance of what she had to tell me. This was in jarring conflict with her entire world-view, which she had been developing and proving to herself for a quarter of a century.

When a therapist and a patient begin speaking with each other there are two immediate dimensions of interaction for each. The first is "how" each is, and the second is "what" they talk about. Sarah's "how" was the superficially compliant (but actually profoundly resistant) way of being in the world that she had developed. For me, the "how" was to intend, as much as I could, to experience just who Sarah was. The "what" she told me will be the subject matter of the next few pages. The "what" for me was the gentle ways I could find to help her look at her view of things in a way that gave her spirit a fair shake. I was hopeful that we would make *contact*.

Six years of consistent, focused psychoanalytic work cannot be reported in a few pages. What follows is a glimpse, much of it in her own words, of what Sarah accomplished during this period. There was roughly a beginning, a middle period and a movement toward separation. Her awareness around many themes: her depression, the impact of her mother's death, her views of her family and her role in it, what was possible for her in the world outside of her family, her sexuality, her relationships with men, particularly Ramon and Paul, her thinking processes, her deep beliefs, the abdication of thinking, which emotions were possible for her and which were forbidden, the chronic affects which haunted her throughout her adult life, the ways she was enmeshed, her fear of abandonment, the interference with her work, the changes that occurred over the years in psychotherapy, all changed over time.

Bereft as she was, like the powerful rumbling of life under the frozen earth in late winter, Sarah's spirit lay ready to burst forward. Most of the lines of music in her personality were frozen solid but they were there, and as she spoke to me over the years they began to thaw. She began to have a recurring dream:

> I'm in an apartment. It is so familiar, yet I can't place it. It was mine, a four-room railroad apartment. I was living in the first room, huddled in the dark and dirt—like my head felt. There was another room I would crawl out into now and again. My sister was in it and Ramon. The last two rooms are lighter, particularly the one at the end. It had a big window. It was filled with light. My sister is walking back and forth saying, do this, do that. I couldn't hear her. Ramon said, "Why don't you move to the back where there is life?"

Her depression first began to lift when she was with me, in our sessions. She was not supposed to feel good with people outside her family. We spent a great deal of time helping her to accept whatever happened between us as all right. We had to constantly keep her focused on her *intention* to get well which initially was accompanied by much anxiety and guilt. Then we had to keep her focused on merely *observing* her life—her behavior, her inner experiences, her unconscious manifestations in dreams and indirect communications. All this time we had to relentlessly drive home the importance of working toward *radical self-acceptance*. She needed to come to realize in an ever-deepening way that whatever she was doing at any particular time represented her best notions of what was necessary for her survival. She was not to berate herself for this, and she was to accept herself even if she did. She was encouraged to stay in her own corner at all costs. Our relationship was in dramatic contrast with her past relationships and kept her off balance. At the same time it provided her with some freedom to move toward being herself.

The unconscious rumblings for life and her inner struggle revealed themselves early in her dreams. She recalled a dream she had the month her mother died, two years before she began psychotherapy.

> I'm in the attic of a house that is filled with people. Suddenly I'm aware that there is a man, dressed all in black with white face and hands, chasing me around the room with a knife. No one in the room seems to notice or care that this man is trying to kill me. I spot Paul in the crowd and ask him if he will stay with me; he stays but offers no further help. The man in black chases me into a deserted corner of the room and is about to stab me.

Six months into therapy she had these dreams.

> I'm lying in my bed at home. At the head of the bed is a window that looks onto the driveway of the neighboring house.

Through the window I see three men standing in the driveway. They can see me, and at first I think they are laughing at me. Suddenly I am outside with them; one of the men grabs me and begins to kiss me. All of a sudden I remember that my mother is in the house (mother had died two years prior); she is terribly sick and is going to die soon. I'm terrified. In a panic I run away.

I'm in the living room of the house with my father and sister. My father says that he is going to have the cats put to sleep. My sister acts indifferent, and says that she really doesn't care, although I know that she does and is only putting on an act to please my father. I am very upset; I must get to a phone to call Dr. McMahon.

This dream is not clear. There were two that were very similar. The surroundings are indistinct, but I am with my family. My mother is very ill; she is emaciated and too weak to move. I'm terrified, for I know that she will die soon. She is sick for a very long time; every day she becomes thinner and weaker, yet she does not die. Finally, I can't stand it any longer. I must get away from it. I leave; I am with other people. In one dream I am having dinner with Maria (the friend who referred her to therapy) and I begin to panic. I remember that my mother is dying; I must go to her. I am terrified that she might already have died. When I get to her I am surprised to find that she is better. She is able to walk around and is looking much better. For a while I am relieved, but then she gets sicker again. She is terribly thin and weak again. She is on the brink of death and I can't stand it. I panic; I must get away.

One of the wonderful things about psychotherapy is that it surfaces the infinite complexity of our inner experience. I think of the operations of the mind as a symphony of six or eight lines of music, so much more rich and full than we, students of the mind, ordinarily consider it to be. But that analogy is just a speck in the infinite and transcendent richness of our psyches. If all of those lines of music are put through prisms and each is shone in an infinite array of colors and subtle tones, it would be something of what is going on inside us all the time. I think of this, sometimes, as I ride the elevator in a high rise building and watch folks strain their necks to follow the numbers, to avoid their self-consciousness, I suppose. I think of the infinite complexity that is simultaneously, and at that very moment, going on in each person. My astonishment at this is explosive.

In you and me and in Sarah, this dazzling mental light show constantly goes on. The dream is such a wonderful hint at this. Each of us has these incredible creative works of art each night. This is who we are! And psychotherapy offers the possibility that some more of this richness other than the narrow destructive piece that has us in its grip will appear. As we begin to inform ourselves of the truth of our inner experience it is frightening, enlightening, exhilarating. When Sarah and I reached the point when she began to *know* what she really knew about her mother, I remember her exclaiming: "This is shocking…this doesn't look good for my mother…did you know all this?"

She began to understand the dynamics of her family. She began to understand the discrepancy between how she was with her family and how she was in the "real world."

> My parents told me that no one should ever become more important than the family—no one should be paid more attention to than the family. Like this business about New Year's Eve; how could I ever want to spend it with someone who will be in and out of my life so quickly and who will take me so lightly. This year my friends know me much better than my family does. *My family only knows a memory of me.*
>
> I'm kind of mad that I spent all those years fighting my normal instincts to be with people. It's wrong. It means you're going to spend your life alone . To my parents, my friends were always "wrong." But they would have liked any of my friends as long as they had nothing to do with me.

I had actually preserved my relationship with my parents by going away. I knew if I went back to Virginia, I couldn't have any friends. They would be threats. They told me that I could live in Virginia and be loved and protected or live in New York and have no friends. Everyone would treat me badly.

Me: In reality, living in New York was the only way you could have friends.

Around this time, in mid-therapy, her sister and her family were scheduled to visit for the first time. Sarah felt apprehensive about this visit because she felt her life was so abnormal, her apartment a mess, etc. I pointed out to her that her uneasiness is a feeling (chronic affect) that is rationalized by those ideas. Actually, because of her parents' injunctions, she has a deep belief that her *success* in New York—that there can be life outside the family—is the problem. She had unconsciously cooperated with the family's attitude that when she leaves Virginia she no longer exists (they never asked her questions about her life in New York, for example), and she is frightened that they will discover that she is actually alive and well outside of Virginia.

At our next appointment she told me about the visit of Joannie and her husband and little Margie. Sarah's voice seemed fuller to me, more mature. She told me that her sister had insulted her. "Ramon pointed it out to me." She stood up to her sister for the first time since they were in junior high school.

All those voices told me I had to side with Joannie over Ramon, but he was right and I didn't listen to them. I told her that she hadn't come to visit me in seven years, that she didn't know me at all and hadn't cared to get to know who I actually was, and she had no business criticizing me, she was my guest.

Ramon met them. It was the first time I told them about having a boy friend that they didn't laugh. I didn't hide Ramon. I didn't hide my life. This is who I am. I even showed her my work. She didn't find it erotic or romantic. It reminded her of death. My sister constantly puts me down. I don't feel intelligent when I talk to her. When I go to Virginia, I totally regress. My father treats me like I'm seventeen, except that at least he speaks to me now. I drop my adult life because I feel so guilty about it. Joannie's adult life is accepted. She was allowed as a kid to "make out" with John in front of them. I couldn't even get a call from a man.

I, too, have been seeing Joannie as she was, not as she is, as adult.

In the next session we worked on the notion that her depression is her *being* her mother, and that her father and sister have a stake in her being that way so that they can symbolically keep mother alive. This is why she reverts to the way she is when she goes "home," and why the family refuses to acknowledge that she has a life of her own in New York. Her depression is her part in maintaining this myth.

She also reported that she got depressed after a fight with Ramon. She is beginning to examine this relationship more carefully. Even though she has gotten a great deal from it she is becoming painfully aware of how limited it is. He refuses to do anything about his addictions; he often doesn't show up when he says he will. She is realizing that his promiscuity is a fear of closeness to her. I pointed out that her choosing to be depressed with an ungiving man is a repetition of how her mother responded to her father. This is when she told me that her father calls her each Saturday evening around 11:30 P.M. She also mentioned that he has been emotionally withholding since her sister saw her apartment. Some weeks later: "My father is panicked about retirement. I got this letter. Told me he is broke because of me. I plunged into the pits of depression, but I got myself out of it.

I reminded Sarah that she is sick to make others well.

> I'm scared to death to stop being depressed around my father. My illness made it possible for my family to function. Joannie used to beat me up and I would give in. If Joannie did-

n't get her way she would have a fit. Mother would get upset, and she would get father upset. The whole family would be a mess if I didn't give in. So, I got depressed.

My father's nuts. He was depressed when he thought he had to retire. Later he blames me for having to work. He claims he hated having to work. I handled him well. I wasn't going to take the blame for the entire madness of my family.

I'm afraid to stop being sick around my father.

Me: Why?

It goes back to when I was young. He went into this rage, and I didn't know why. What he attacked was the beginning of my independent behavior. My sister did the same thing and she wasn't in trouble. *If I was sick he left me alone.* If I got better, he began to criticize.

I'm afraid to let him see what I'm like. I'm afraid that if I told him I went away and found out I was all right, his guilt would make him sick. I get anxious and fearful lest they withdraw from me . His perception of reality is so off so he has things reversed.

Me: That is some kettle of fish. What do you do when you discover a parent doesn't want what's best for you?

It's a mortal sin to tell anyone anything about my family. My role in my family must change. I don't want any of us to be sick any more.

Another time:

Why did I feel so guilty about changing when I came here?

Me: Because it was too separate, too different than your parents.

Yes, yes (animatedly)…that's it…very good…it was too separate. At the beginning I would tell them what I was doing but, as time went on, it was too different, too separate. I think I'm mad at my mom. I've been thinking this recently.

Me: Doesn't that make you feel guilty?

Yes…I've known for months, but I've felt too guilty to tell you. This doesn't look good for my mother, but I've got to get into it. [Sarah changes the subject. I pointed this out.]

My mother was getting the wrong medication, so it made her very angry. My boy friend, Harry, would leave and she would scream at me, traumatize me. Any time any boy called me there was a scene in the house. I would go to my room and play my music. Songs are very important to me…Joannie Mitchell…"Ladies of the Canyon"…Leonard Cohen…you know, depressed stuff. My parents hated it and would yell at me…wow, I just remembered…when I was seeing Paul I didn't listen to popular music either. He was like my parents. They hated popular music.

After several years of psychotherapy, Sarah began to develop a fuller, richer, more complete viewpoint toward her parents and her sister. The reason this is so is that each of us has very rich and complicated emotional and intellectual "takes" on the significant people in our lives, particularly our families. All of this study of them is not to assign blame. Rather it is to expand our insights into the people in our lives who have deeply influenced us, not to find the "bad guys." One's love of oneself is a carefully honed thing, won in hand-to-hand combat with oneself, not with any other. The importance of becoming aware of a more complete perception is not to rest smugly and content as a victim, but rather to find space around our spirits to move forward in whatever way we choose.

The beginning of the process of achieving a more accurate view of our caretakers and letting go of deep beliefs is generally quite upsetting. Sometimes it is a hard and fixed, angry view of a parent that begins to yield to a more loving and compassionate one. This may be difficult, as well. For whatever the viewpoints we have developed in our childhood, they seemed to us to be crucial to our very existence. "If they see me as independent and happy they will abandon me," cries Sarah. With that deep belief, the expansion into a more complete take on life almost always is immersed in fear and sadness and even anguish.

In this process we will encounter profound emotions and make tentative judgments, and this is good. We are letting *ourselves* see, and whether we are "right" or "wrong," this commitment to our own view is wisdom.

Over the next few years Sarah continued to develop wisdom.

> I feel that I am not supposed to be "real" with other people; "real" is the way I now feel. I have been shadowy, detached when I'm with others. It's one aspect of depression, separate from just mood. The difference in the way I feel is extreme; it's like being in a whole other dimension. For the past six years I have been emotionally dead (out of "contact").
>
> I feel guilty when I try to break through this "invisible barrier." I panic when I begin to feel "real" with other people. I'm only supposed to be real with members of my family. Like in childhood, I expect disaster when I become "real." Being "real" is only the way other people are normally, but I am not supposed to be that way (in "contact").
>
> I feel *angry* that I am not allowed to be real. I am perceiving (wrongly) that all people I know are involved in some kind of conspiracy to keep me from being normal. It's as if they are saying, "If you become normal I won't have anything to do with you; other people can be normal and have relationships but you can't! I become angry, depressed, but terrified that if I ever show my feelings I will be abandoned. All this has made me feel hopeless about relationships.
>
> Other people can be used as an "out." If they are sufficiently domineering they will try to run my life (Paul) and thus relieve me of the responsibility and guilt. For years I was terrified that Paul would leave me although I knew I didn't love him and even wanted to get away. *The fear is almost that if they leave me I will cease to exist on some level.* I am always fighting paralyses when alone. Some terror is pursuing me and I am always trying to escape it. When I was involved with Paul I felt that if he left me

I would never go out again. You said it was loyalty. It is, but not to Paul. It's a misguided loyalty to my parents.

At a later time she told me:

> None of these insights have come to me accidentally. There are reasons. The timing was very important. It's not accidental that I went into this depression in mid-January of 1979 (my mother entered the hospital in mid-January of 1978). These insights started *coming to me* in mid-January. It is no accident that these came to me when I was with Ramon; no accident that they always came to me after or during making love. I hesitated to tell you. First, I feel guilty about Ramon and the fact that we have sex stoned. But I also feel guilty about sex, really the intensity of my sexual feelings for him.
>
> It was very important that I did not sense any disapproval on your part of my relationship with Ramon. *Ramon is a very important person in my life. You are the first person to acknowledge this.* I was happy with Ramon. I cared about him, and he cared about me. But I felt it was bad. He's black, he drinks, he takes drugs, he's unfaithful, and he has no thoughts of marrying me. He's irresponsible, but in reality I learned the truth about myself and my life with him.

Toward the end of our work she had these deep understandings about her depression:

> There is a link between my mother and depression that goes back to very early childhood. It is connected to *a very early fear of desertion*—the loss of my mother's love. I think that an early interaction may have been this. My depression enabled my mother to be happy—depression increases feelings of helplessness, which may have in turn *stimulated my mother to be more concerned and loving.* Conversely, my happiness may have been more difficult for my mother to deal with—I would have been more active, less quiet, and she may have responded to this by

becoming depressed herself. This would necessarily result in a diminished ability to give me love. I may have felt terrified at this perceived loss of my mother's love and responded by becoming depressed. Thus, a very early connection was probably formed between my being depressed and receiving love. *Love is lost when I am happy.*

Fear of separation—the loss of love triggers immediate and very deep responses of depression. It is as if by becoming depressed I will regain the lost love. There is a very deep connection between depression, *being good,* and receiving love.

She returns to the theme of necessity of being good, but before that she speaks of her father:

My early memories of my father are that I loved him. My first depression when I was 12, I think, had to do with the loss of my father's love. I clung to my mother which further reinforced the depressive reaction. I perceived that my father stopped loving me because I was bad. I was bad because I had experienced loving, sexual feelings toward men other than him. His problems caused him to go into an intense rage. I think that the problem was sexual. To this day he cannot acknowledge that I have ever had any relationship with a man. I feel he automatically hates all men that I know—including you.

All these feelings have been repressed since I was 12. When my mother was dying all these feelings began to resurface. My mother was dying and my father didn't love me. He would disappear entirely if he knew what I had done (sexual guilt). I must be very good (depressed) or else he will leave, too. Above all I must have no relationships or emotions for anyone other than my family.

There is a very early connection between being depressed and being good. Things that make me *happy* are *bad.* Playing with other children made me happy but it was bad. My early romantic feelings made me happy but were bad. I do bad things when I am happy. My feelings for Ramon are bad and therefore I must deny their very existence.

I must not care about anyone else and *I must not allow them to care about me.* People like me when I am happy, and that's bad. I must keep denying that anyone cares about me.

Around this time she had this telling dream:

> I am in a group of people who are about to explore a very old house/castle/museum. It's a very important exploration, for the house has been vacant for many, many years. Pictures are to be done by one member of the group (a young woman who reminds me of a "straight" friend of mine from City College). Actually, I am in charge of the Art work (which is a record of the journey) but she will be doing all the initial art work. I resent it a little but must grudgingly admit that she does do lovely drawings. Anyway, I will be doing all the organizing and finishing touches. The group has a leader, but I am not able to see him. The only recognizable member of the group is a black man, whom I have sexual feelings for. I know that I will get to know him. The young woman who reminds me of my conservative friend is such a good person. I ought to be more like her. She will enter the house first. I'm afraid to go because the house is dark and scary. It is filled with spiders and cobwebs. I will go. She will enter first, but I will follow.
>
> The two women are me. The young woman is how I think I should be. It is also me now—depressed but good (good in relation to my parents). She is also unreal—remote and distant. She lacks the warmth and depth of a real person. Myself in the dream represents me with all the different aspects of my personality. The black man is Ramon. The leader of the group is you. The expedition is therapy, and the scary house is my mind. The artwork is the work I'm doing now which is also a form of therapy.

I am coming to the end of telling you about Sarah and our work together, and I am noticing a sadness in me. I am going through other material, criticizing myself for not including it. It is clear that I don't want to conclude this chapter. My studying my notes and re-experiencing Sarah have opened my memories and feelings about her, and I have to separate from her once again.

Toward the end we spent more time speaking of our relationship. Once she overslept and missed an appointment. The next time we met she was terrified that I would be angry, and she would get depressed. On a deep level she felt she would be abandoned, once again, if she didn't do things "my way." "I want you to have all your feelings," I told her. "Anger is good. It tells you a lot about the world. It is no problem if I am angry or if you are angry. We do not have to hurt each other or leave each other because of it."

The final struggle with me, of course, would be about leaving, about terminating psychotherapy, and she managed to accomplish this as well. Somewhat peremptorily, perhaps, but leaving is very hard as we saw above. It is hard for each of us, for the therapist as well as the patient. Termination of a long, intimate relationship, even if for the purpose of healing, is not always the therapist's finest hour. But we managed it, somewhat bungled though it may have been. It is better, of course, not to leave therapy a moment before it is time. It is equally important not to remain a moment *after* it is time, and we therapists, I'm afraid, often err in this regard, though it is not always easy to know. We have to end a love relationship, too. No matter how well a person is doing, there remains the crucial task of separating from the therapist and living on one's own for the full, safe experience of self. She has to leave perhaps the best, fullest, most caring true contact she has ever known.

So Sarah busted out. Before she did she made major shifts in many areas of her life. She outgrew Ramon. As much as she loved him, he was not getting better, and she was. She wanted more. She began to date. She began to enjoy men. "Is it bad to be cheered up about this [referring to mens' interest in her]?" "I really enjoy men." She developed a clear understanding of what her relationships with Ramon and with Paul were all about. She learned how to appraise the new people who came into her life, accurately and quickly. "I don't have to immediately become what they want." "I no longer become what people say I am."

She developed relationships with women. "My mother never had any women friends." She felt allowed to do this and began to process the world with the aid of the perception of female friends. If a girlfriend disagreed with her about something, a man for example, she tended to defer to this person as she did to her mother. But Sarah increasingly learned and got better at sticking up for herself.

Her work blossomed. She worked regularly and with power and began to show it to others. She began to sell. Her work became more a function of her spirit than her fusion with mother. She was able to grasp the heretofore horrible notion that at times parents can be envious and jealous and even, out of their own neurotic needs, sabotage what is best for their children. And she could come to forgive them. "If my mother had had help she would have been capable of seeing these things. Her love and understanding would have been in no way diminished—*but her behavior would have changed in such a way as to allow us both to become healthier people.*"

The final obstacle, as I mentioned, was her body. Often the final defense of the demons, her body and appearance were attacked. Her hair became matted; she was filled with yeast. It felt like there were bugs in her skin. Here, too, patient acceptance on both our sides was helpful. It took a long time. It was discouraging, because she had made so many changes in all areas of her life and now this! Was it all to no purpose? in vain? We persevered. We stayed in emotional contact through her desperation. She took all the steps possible to deal with the physical expressions of her conflicts. She sought out alternative medical strategies. At the same time I was relentless in the defense of her spirit, constantly pointing out to her that it was her obedience to her parents that kept her ill, at least in part. It was her guilt at stepping out on her own. She was eating of the fruit of the tree of the knowledge of good and evil. She was leaving the paradise of her parents' love and protection. She was becoming herself.

And then she left. When I received her letter I wrote back:

Dear Sarah,

I can't tell you how happy I was to get your letter. Your news is exciting and touched me deeply. Although I am an optimist (cockeyed, perhaps!) by nature and although I believe deeply in the basic goodness of the universe and that things are more or less unfolding as they should, sometimes that conviction is severely challenged—this past week is a good example. (Note: I was referring to the war in the Persian Gulf.)

And then, Low and behold, your note arrives. Yes, I always believed in you but sometimes I question myself. I wondered whether I could have done more—or, perhaps, something different. But your success doesn't shock me. I'm never surprised when a person I know to be a beautiful spirit achieves happiness. With all its madness, life is good. Thanks for reminding me.

When you get in town, give me a ring—if only to say, "hello."

Fondly,

Jim

What was it about our work that was helpful to Sarah?

To begin with, I didn't judge her. I saw her not as a failure or a wrong-doer. On the contrary, I considered her very courageous, a person who had come very far despite severe obstacles. Even at her most "disabled," I admired her courage in persevering each day against tremendous odds and with little hope. From the outset, I thought of her as quite a piece of work! Perhaps that attitude, although not frequently articulated, permeated our work and was healing to her. *Her* attitude and intention, too, was very important. She wanted to get well. Her spirit had not surrendered and so she was able to absorb my caring and find sustenance in it. If it were not for her deep desire to "grow out," she would have run from a person who was devoted to her prosperity.

Although I was committed to her accomplishing her goals, whatever they were, and certainly to her finding peace and joy, on a deep level I accepted Sarah exactly as she was when I met her. I was not afraid. This is in contrast to a psychiatrist she consulted who wanted to treat her with heavy doses of medication and possibly some kind of institutionalization. Sarah experienced a regression after this encounter. Her demons used it to rant at her that this expert's advice was definite proof of her worthlessness. For whatever reason, I saw it differently. I saw her illness as a place she needed to be for the moment. She was commencing a journey into wholeness, a radical and dramatic rejection of the false self and the false life she had felt forced to create. So it was not a failure, this "illness," but a jumping-off point, and it had to be honored as such. When the psychiatrist told me that she would continue to try to influence Sarah to undergo heavy psychotropic medication and enter a sheltered workshop program, I told her that I would treat this advice as I would any other bad influence on Sarah and work with it therapeutically. Sarah laughed when I told her this; her negative feelings about herself, triggered by her contact with the psychiatrist, began to lift and we continued our work together. I had to search my heart about this as well. Should I let her be so treated? It certainly would "cover" myself. Not really. "Covering" oneself is the most dangerous thing a person can do in the long run because it is a rejection of truth, and truth is always our first ally in life. Intuitively, I sensed that what would be good for me as well as Sarah (and hopefully, the psychiatrist) would be to remain with Sarah, by her emotional side, in her journey.

I was also not judgmental about some of her behavior, particularly about her relationship with Ramon. Common wisdom, and certainly that of her girlfriends, was that Ramon was an exploiter, a drug addict who was taking advantage of this poor, sick, pretty young woman for sex and money. This is certainly a reasonable point of view. But Ramon was more than this. He, too, was sick, and at the same time saw something life-affirming in Sarah. Their relationship was characterized by moments of real intimacy. They were lost souls, but they loved each other and contacted each other, each in a courageous way if courage is considered behaving against the injunctions of your early caretakers. Sarah hung in with him, risking the terror of the abandoning disapproval of her family. She had an intimate friend other than family! She was wildly sexual! She was open to the new both in behavior and in the depths of their mutual emotional exploration. For his part, Ramon stayed much longer than *his* friends would have counseled. He went to new emotional places with Sarah; he did the best he could. He grew enormously. With all its problems, their relationship had the poignancy of Romeo and Juliet. When Sarah was ready to let him go it was not with a sense of having been abused, but rather, sadly, that she had outgrown him but would always be grateful to him for his kindness, total acceptance, and in his way, loyalty. Without romanticizing the relationship, I did communicate my understanding of the growth I believe it represented. She experienced this as a powerful affirmation of her growth impulse.

There are many theories of how psychological change occurs in psychotherapy, but the reality is we just don't know for sure. As we have seen, there are some things that seem to correlate with it. Certainly the training and experience of the psychotherapist is important. But so is the patient's finding deep within the courage to take a chance. Sarah spoke of her inner experience freely and courageously. She spoke of her memories, her deepest beliefs and convictions, even at the times when she believed they didn't make sense. She dreamt, and she told me her dreams. Between sessions she would write these things down, and at my suggestion, bring them in to me. She presented all of her life for observation, despite the feelings and pain that often accompanied them. And she did this even though she often was depressed and discouraged. Each of us took the risk of true contact and in doing so we were able to look at just how she was stuck. We examined all the ways her demons tried to get her to resist opening up to me. We analyzed her feelings about me, how they interfered with our work, what clues they provided to her deepest beliefs, thought patterns, emotions. Together we articulated all the ways she was enmeshed in her family, particularly the *deepest* belief that previously forbade her from even looking for a way out. As she did this over the years her mood changed, her energy increased; she became clearer. She began to accept herself more and then created her relationships to fit with this new acceptance. She began to share her gift—she began to work.

The reason that in some basic way we do not truly know how psychotherapy effects change is that we just do not know enough of how human beings function in many significant ways. How do we measure Sarah's desire to grow, her hanging in there when all seemed lost? How to understand the love of the therapist, the place in him that is tapped by the courage of the other so that the two engage in this powerful, passionate, absorbing, spiritual work yet have no other involvement in each other's life? What is known is that Sarah came and hung in there and told it all, and I accepted and loved and shared my observations with her. And the miracle of growth occurred.

The last contact I have had with her as of this writing was her response to my letter:

February 2, 1991

Dear Jim,

Thanks so much for your kind letter! I can never repay you for everything you did for me; believe me, when I had no one else to turn to, *it helped*. I'll stay in touch and hope to see you the next time we're in New York. (Perhaps I can even come in for a regular appointment, just for old times' sake.)

Things here continue good. I have a circle of friends now many of whom are sitting for me for portraits. I'm able to go outside and work (an "iffy" business in the city). Of course, Ted and I, like you, are unhappy about this wretched war. Ted organized a teach in at his college; the huge attendance suggests that many other people feel as we do. Let's hope.

Thanks again, and our very best, as always.

Your friend,

Sarah Maloney (Larson)

Notes

(1) Miller, A. *Drama of The Gifted Child,* originally titled *Prisoners of Childhood* (New York: Basic Books, 1981)

7

The Future of the Courageous Psychotherapist

In thinking of my parting words to you, my friends in the extended family of psychotherapy and psychoanalysis, two images come to mind. The first is a scene in the dance movie, "Carmen," in which the director, Antonio Gades, exhorts his exhausted dancers to continue the passionate contact with the earth that is flamenco—each of them dripping with sweat, each face contorted with deep fatigue and pain. Dancing with them amidst the pounding and frenzy of the electrifying music, he shouts, "ENDURE!"

The other image is a sign on the back of a local utility truck in New York, which reads, "112 years of consistent reliable service…A good beginning!"

That is what we psychotherapists need—to endure, and to realize that after about 112 years we, too, have made a good beginning. But just a beginning.

One of our biggest mistakes has been that in our hubris we have proclaimed from the beginning that we are at the end, and it was almost the end of us. No, we are at the beginning, and what we need more than anything is Beginner's Mind, that wonderful Buddhist counsel that encourages each of us to empty our spirit of ego at the end of the day and start anew the following one with the innocence of children, the children that Jesus invites to come to him. Because Jesus-wisdom and

Buddha enlightenment come on those days when we start fresh and let the truth of the universe that lives in each one of us slowly seep up into our consciousness. We can then meet the day and ourselves and each other with freshness and delight.

Still, beginners or no, we have certainly learned truths about how people grow and how we go astray and how we work intrapsychically, and we have found some remedies that help folks get back on track, to begin to return to themselves. Resistance, transference, the untapped depths of the unconscious, dynamic motivation, defense mechanisms, repression, denial—chief among them even in the not so crazy of us. These are great discoveries. You can add your own to this list.

I, of course, would add the importance of intensity of contact, of presence, of the deep understanding of fusion, the appreciation of shared pain as a cure for shame, of the necessity of deep feeling. Of humility. I believe that the sharing of pain in love is the remedy for everything that ails us. And that kindness can suffuse it all, starting with kindness to oneself.

Not only do we know these things, but we must fight to keep them in the world's awareness, because we live in a time of dangerous denial of these truths. Disheartened by the shocking ignorance of the very notion of unconscious processes on the part of his Literature graduate students, Professor Mark Edmunson (1) writes, "Our human dignity, Freud says, does not come from trying to overcome all that is natural in us—drives, dreams, emotions. We can never still the war that rages inside. We need to own up to the turbulence of the psyche and live with it. For their own well-being, my students—and I—need to entertain the possibility that we can desire what we are also repulsed by, that love takes strange, sometimes inscrutable paths, that we don't always know what it is we're up to. The world into which Freud introduced his work was in many ways a blinkered place where people believed that they had evolved beyond the claims of nature. The danger is that in trying to leave Freud behind, we will become pre-Freudians again." Physiologist Jared Diamond (2), writing in Natural History magazine, in contrasting the current attitudes toward

Freud and Darwin, whom he considers equal in their genius and impact on the world, points out the Freud bashing that is rampant these days." The other type of Freud bashing—much more damaging because it hurts patients—comes from a too-narrow focus on biological psychiatry...to my mind, academe's swing from talk therapies is tragic. Major advances are still being made in this field...Almost all of us face stress in our jobs, our health, our personal relationships, and our own aspirations. Almost all of us carry emotional and cognitive baggage from our early lives that leaves us with some inappropriate responses in our lives as adults. Some problems require professional distance, experience, and skills—the skills in which a talk therapist is trained and that are far beyond the capacity of a friend to deliver." But these are voices in the wilderness. We psychotherapists and our patients are the pilgrims who carry the truth of human psychic functioning in this regressed, repressed, "blinkered" time.

While much of the world is in denial, if we are passionate about our calling, we are truly "conquistadors." For the true, unique self gestates in the not yet known parts of us. It bubbles up in that part of our personality, a very deep, deep line of our music which remains outside of societal convention. Our activities within convention, such as being a spouse or a professor may have been the result of our creations outside of convention. But our actual spousing and professoring is now in the automatic part of us, the great commonweal of life. It is separate from the growing and co-creating that remains deep within our self, that part of us that is still being pushed by spirit into unknown realms, ever deepening levels of reality, places of which we ourselves are ignorant and even afraid. Here is where the battle between spirit and demon continues and where growth perseveres, the only place where true growth, "unique expression rather than mere achievement," is born.

So we must be a little wary of "health" and adjustment and accomplishment, as Joyce McDougall cautions us. And most of all we must respect that part of us that still struggles, for therein lives creation, even if the fruits of that creation still are mere "drafts." We must be patient with ourselves, because we have the unique human problem of awareness, and so we have to watch all our success, after it is over, slide quickly into a sort of bin of death. The result is the necessity to be born again into chaos and confusion and ignorance, and start all over—if we are to grow. But worst of all is self-complacency, because then we have settled for mere success rather than the challenge of living until we die. If we appreciate this, radical self-acceptance becomes not a begrudging affirmation of our worth, a good spirited hurrah to ourselves as we plod along in life, but rather a deep insight and respect for what is perhaps the finest part of ourselves, though often the messiest and least rewarded by "the world."

Notes

(1) Edmundson, M. "Magazine Section" *New York Times*, 7/13/1997
(2) Diamond, Jared, *Natural History,* 2/2001

References

Alexander, F.M. *The Use of the Self.* Long Beach, Calif.: Centerline Press, 1985; originally published New York: E.P.Dutton, 1932.

Barzini, L. *The Italians* (Atheneum, 1964)

Bayley, J. *Elegy for Iris* (New York: St. Martin's Press, 1999)

Bernstein, A. "Lecture to the Fellows of the American Institute of Psychotherapy and Psychoanalysis" (New York: 1992)

Cahill, T. *How the Irish Saved Civilization*, Bantam Doubleday Dell Publishing Group, 3/1996

Cocks, G. *Psychotherapy in the Third Rich: The Goering Institute* (Oxford University Press, 1980)

Crisp, Q. *Sunday Tea with Quentin Crisp* (P.S. 1 Performance Space, 10/18/92)

Edmundson, M. "Magazine Section" *New York Times*, 7/13/1997

Diamond, Jared, *Natural History,* 2/2001

Egan T. N.Y. Times Op-Ed page (9/16/93)

Eisely, L. *Immense Journey* (New York: Vintage Books, 1959)

Freud, S. "The Question of Lay Analysis" in *Standard Edition* (Hogarth Press, 1957), 20:251-260

_____. "Postscript on the Question of Lay Analysis" in *Standard Edition* (Hogarth Press, 1957), 20:251-260

Itsuki, Hiroyuki. *Tariki.* (Tokyo: Kodanshka Ltd: 2001) p.xvii

Joyce, J.T. *New Yorker, 9/4/98*

Karen, R. "Shame." *Atlantic Monthly* (February 1992), 40-70

Kurtz, E. *Shame and Guilt: Characteristics of the Dependency Cycle* (Hazelden Press 1981)

Levine, S. *Who Dies? An investigation of conscious living and conscious dying* (Basic Books, 1982)

Masson, J. *The Assault on Truth: Freud's Suppression of the Seduction Theory,* Pocket Books, 9/1998

McDougall, J. *A Plea for a Measure of Abnormality.* (New York: International University Press, 1980)

McMahon, J. *The Price of Wisdom.* (New York: Crossroad Press, 1996)*

_____ *Letting Go of Mother.* (New York / Mahwah, N.J.: Paulist Press, 1996)*

_____ *Radical Self-Acceptance.* (New York: Crossroad Press, 1999)*

Miller, A. *Drama of The Gifted Child* originally titled *Prisoners of Childhood* (New York: Basic Books,. 1981)

Morita, S. *Shinkeishitsu No Hontai To Ryoho [Nature of Neurosis and Its Therapy].* (Tokyo: Hakuyosha, 1983)

Racker, H. *Transference and Countertransference* (Hogarth Press, 1968)

Reynolds, D. *The Quiet Therapies: Japanese Pathways to Personal Growth.* (Honolulu: Hawaii, 1980)

Roth, P. *American Pastoral* (New York: Houghton Mifflin, 1997)

Schachtel, E. *Metamorphosis* (New York: Basic Books, 1959)

Singer, I.B. Interview, *Time Magazine,* circa 1993

Stoller, R. *Sex and Gender* (Science House, 1968)

Strachey, J. "The Nature of the Therapeutic Action of Psychoanalysis," in *The Evolution of Psychoanalytic Technique.* eds. M. Bergmann and F. Hartman. (Basic Books, 1976)

Wilson, A. Op-Ed page *N.Y. Times,* 5/12/1996

* For more of the author's works see **www.jamesmcmahonphd.com/**

0-595-22635-3